PET *Masterclass*

Intermediate

Student's Book

Annette Capel

Rosemary Nixon

OXFORD

UNIVERSITY PRESS

Contents

Introducing PET   6

		READING	WRITING	LISTENING
Module 1 Introduction	**7**			
1.1 The same routine	8	**Part 3** Correct / incorrect sentences	Correcting mistakes	
1.2 Different experiences	10			Handling long recordings
2.1 Sales power	12	**Part 1** Understanding adverts		
2.2 Are you a shopaholic?	14		Using correct punctuation	**Part 4** Matching opinions to speaker
3.1 Aches and pains	16			**Part 1** Identifying what is in the pictures
3.2 Staying healthy	18	**Part 2** Understanding the people descriptions	Choosing the correct verb form	
4.1 Perfect homes	20	**Part 5** Parts of speech		
4.2 Home from home	22		Using informal language	**Part 3**
Module 1 Review	24			
Module 2 Introduction	**27**			
5.1 Waste not, want not	28	**Part 4** Understanding writer purpose	**Part 1**	
5.2 What's it like there?	30		**Part 3 Letter** EXAM TASK Describing a place	**Part 1** Identifying location
6.1 Go for gold	32			**Part 2** Answering multiple-choice questions
6.2 Sport for all	34	**Part 2** Identifying words and phrases with similar meanings	**Part 2** EXAM TASK Identifying functions of sentences	
7.1 Body fuel	36	**Part 4** Matching questions to options		
7.2 Special recipes	38		**Part 3 Story** EXAM TASK Sequencing linkers	**Part 4** Identifying opinions and facts
8.1 Old building, new use	40	**Part 3** Finding sentences with similar meaning		
8.2 State of the art	42	**Part 5**	**Part 1** EXAM TASK Spelling rules	**Part 3** Predicting type of answer
Module 2 Review	44			
Module 3 Introduction	**47**			
9.1 Internet interests	48	**Part 2** Looking for similar information	**Part 2** Answering each point of the task	
9.2 Leisure interests	50			**Part 1** Identifying subject of recordings
10.1 Summer music	52	**Part 5** EXAM TASK		**Part 2** Predicting text content
10.2 Screen scene	54		**Part 3 Letter** Planning a letter	

SPEAKING	GRAMMAR	VOCABULARY
Talking about routines	Uncountable nouns	Daily life
Discussion	Past simple and past continuous	Phrasal verbs with *get* and *give*
Talking about advertising	Comparisons	Adjectives and adverbs
Talking about shopping		Shopping, clothes Verbs connected with clothes
Talking about healthy lifestyles	Ability and possibility	Parts of the body Illnesses and health
Persuading people of benefits		
Talking about people's homes		Rooms and furniture Order of adjectives
	Imperatives	
Part 3 Giving an opinion and reasons	The passive	Prefixes *re-* and *non-*
		Describing places Weather
Talking about sports	Present simple and present continuous Adverbs of frequency	Sport
Parts 3 and 4		
	Conditional clauses with *if / unless*	Quantifiers
Talking about food **Parts 3 and 4** Preparing to speak		Food and drink
Part 2	Present perfect	Places and buildings Suffixes *-ful* and *-able*
Part 4 Discussion	Relative pronouns	Verbs of movement
Talking about the internet	Verbs and prepositions followed by *-ing*	
Part 3 Making and responding to suggestions		Hobbies and interests
Talking about music festivals	Obligation and prohibition	Music
Part 3 Describing location and people in a photograph		Films *-ed* and *-ing* adjectives Descriptive adjectives

		READING	WRITING	LISTENING
11.1 Take the challenge	56	**Part 3** Checking information		
11.2 Take a break	58		Linking words	**Part 3** Predicting type of answer
12.1 Different relationships	60	**Part 1** Messages	**Part 1**	**Part 4** EXAM TASK
12.2 Close to you	62		**Part 3 Story** Continuing from first sentence Including adverbs	
Module 3 Review	64			
Module 4 Introduction	67			
13.1 Your own wheels	68	**Part 4** EXAM TASK	**Part 2** Using your own words	
13.2 On the move	70			**Part 1** EXAM TASK
14.1 Free to talk	72	**Part 5**	**Part 3 Letter** Keeping to the task	
14.2 Disappearing languages	74			**Part 2** EXAM TASK
15.1 At your service	76			**Part 3** Spelling
15.2 Student life	78	**Part 2** EXAM TASK	**Part 2** Writing varied sentence openings	
16.1 It could happen to you...	80	**Part 1** Understanding detailed meaning		
16.2 Life can be difficult	82		**Part 3 Story** Identifying a suitable title	**Part 4** Understanding detailed meaning
Module 4 Review	84			
Module 5 Introduction	87			
17.1 The working world	88			**Part 1** Identifying what type of information to listen for
17.2 All work and no play	90	**Part 3** EXAM TASK	**Part 2** Keeping a message short	
18.1 Fame	92			**Part 2** Giving reasons for your answers
18.2 Glittering prizes	94	**Part 5**	**Part 3 Letter** Avoiding repetition	
19.1 In captivity	96	**Part 4** Global meaning	**Part 1**	
19.2 In the wild	98		**Part 3 Story** Endings	**Part 3** EXAM TASK
20.1 Get ready!	100	**Part 1** EXAM TASK		
20.2 Aim high!	102		**Part 3 Letter** Maximising marks	**Part 4** Verbs expressing attitude or opinion
Module 5 Review	104			

Additional materials 107–108   PET Exam guide 109–120   Vocabulary reference 121–125   Grammar reference 126–135

SPEAKING	GRAMMAR	VOCABULARY
	Past simple and past perfect	Verb–noun phrases
Talking about holidays **Part 2** EXAM TASK		Travel and holidays
	Reported speech	Relationships Adjective–preposition phrases
Part 4 Examples and discussion		Phrasal verbs
Part 1	*Will / shall*	Transport Prepositional phrases
Parts 3 and 4 Talking about preferences and reasons		Confused words
	Used to	Language and customs
Talking about services **Part 3** How to describe things without knowing the exact words	*Have / get* something done	Services
Talking about study preferences	Future forms	
Part 1 EXAM TASK	Second conditional	
		Affixes *un-* and *-less*
Part 2 Agreeing and disagreeing	Infinitives	Words connected with *employ*
Talking about work		
Parts 3 and 4 EXAM TASKS		Compound adjectives
	Quantity *some / any / every / no*	
Part 4 Discussion	*So do I* *Neither / nor do I*	
		Animals Verbs with prepositions
Part 2	Possessive forms	
		Words connected with *attention* Suffixes *-ation* and *-ment*

Introducing PET

PET, the Preliminary English Test, corresponds to level B1 of the *Common European Framework* and is based on the *Threshold Level* specification (1990, Council of Europe). All four skills of reading, writing, listening and speaking are assessed, each skill accounting for 25% of the total marks available.

PET tests the language used in everyday situations through a range of different test formats, and covers the range of topics needed for basic understanding and communication in English, for example, daily life; education; entertainment and media; health, medicine and exercise; places and buildings; shopping; travel and holidays, and so on.

Candidates take three papers: Paper 1 Reading and Writing, Paper 2 Listening, and Paper 3 Speaking. They do not necessarily have to pass all three components, since their final mark is a total score across the three. There are two passing grades, *Pass with merit* and *Pass*, and two failing grades, *Narrow fail* and *Fail*. *Pass* is around 70% of the total marks and *Pass with merit* around 85%.

The March 2004 PET Update has introduced minor changes across all four skills, but the most significant changes are within the Writing component. Here, candidates are now tested on their ability to show grammatical accuracy at sentence level, to produce a short communicative message, and to write an extended piece of English – candidates can choose either a story or an informal letter.

The Cambridge ESOL website, www.cambridge-esol.org, offers further information on PET, including an annual Examination Report.

Paper 1 Reading and Writing (1 hour 30 minutes)

This paper carries 50% of the final marks. In the Reading component, 35 marks are scaled to 25%. For the Writing, 15 marks are available for Part 3 and 5 marks each for Parts 1 and 2.

Reading

Part 1 Notices and messages (multiple choice)
Test focus: understanding real world notices and short communicative messages

Part 2 People descriptions and short texts (matching)
Test focus: reading for specific information and detailed comprehension

Part 3 Factual text (true / false)
Test focus: reading for specific information and ignoring redundant material

Part 4 Attitude / opinion text (multiple choice)
Test focus: recognising writer purpose; reading for gist, inference and global meaning

Part 5 Short text (multiple choice)
Test focus: reading for general meaning; understanding vocabulary and grammar

Writing

Part 1 Sentence transformations
Test focus: showing control and understanding of grammatical structures and lexico-structural patterns; reformulating information

Part 7 Short communicative message (35–45 words)
Test focus: demonstrating the ability to communicate content and ideas clearly and concisely

Part 8 Continuous writing (about 100 words)
Test focus: writing an extended answer, showing control and range of language

Paper 2 Listening (about 30 minutes + 6 minutes to transfer answers)

This paper has a total possible mark of 25. Candidates hear each part twice.

Part 1 Short monologues and dialogues (multiple choice)
Test focus: listening to identify key information

Part 2 Longer monologue or 'prompted' interview (multiple choice)
Test focus: listening to identify specific information and detailed meaning

Part 3 Longer monologue (gap fill)
Test focus: listening to identify and interpret information, in order to complete notes or sentences

Part 4 Longer dialogue (true / false)
Test focus: listening for detailed meaning and to identify attitudes and opinions

Paper 3 Speaking (10–12 minutes per pair)

This paper has a total possible mark of 25.

Part 1 Factual and personal information (2–3 minutes)
Test focus: giving information and spelling a name (the examiner asks each candidate some questions)

Part 2 Simulated situation (2–3 minutes)
Test focus: using appropriate functional language to carry out a task, with a visual stimulus (the two candidates interact)

Part 3 Extended turn (3 minutes)
Test focus: responding to photos and managing discourse in a long turn (each candidate is given a photograph and asked to talk about it)

Part 4 General conversation (3 minutes)
Test focus: discussing the topic raised in Part 3 (the two candidates interact and are if necessary prompted with additional questions by the interlocutor)

Topics

1 What topics do the pictures show?

Vocabulary

2 Which pictures are these shown in?

bandage   doctor   plate   shaving
goods   terrace   washing up   website

Grammar

3 Match sentences 1–4 to a grammar area a–d and underline the words that show you this.

1 Clare's new flat is bigger than her last one.

2 Joe might buy another car – he's thinking about an old sports car.

3 Brush your teeth twice a day if you want to keep them healthy.

4 I overslept yesterday and then everything went wrong.

a   verbs of possibility
b   imperatives
c   comparisons
d   past tenses

1.1 The same routine

Warm up

→ VOCABULARY REFERENCE PAGE 121

1 Where are the people in the photos? What are they doing? Do you think they have the same routine every day?

2 In pairs, discuss your own daily routine. Is it always the same? Does it change at the weekend? Find three things you both do every day and something different you each do at the weekend.

3 What are the advantages of having a daily routine? What are the disadvantages?

Reading

4 Read the article, stopping after every paragraph. For each paragraph, say which sentence is correct and which is incorrect.

5 Do you think the article offers good advice? Why / Why not?

6 Match underlined words 1–8 in the article to their meaning (A or B).

1	sensible	A	wise	B	particular
2	vary	A	keep	B	change
3	simple	A	basic	B	crazy
4	physical	A	active	B	scientific
5	essential	A	important	B	perfect
6	calm	A	silence	B	peace
7	poor	A	cheap	B	bad
8	worries	A	fears	B	difficulties

Learning to listen to **yourself**

Have you ever done something just because it 'felt right' – or refused to do something because it felt wrong? Learning to take your body's advice seems <u>sensible</u>, yet many people aren't confident enough to live like this. In order to feel safe, they do the same things every day. But that's how people get stuck and fail to enjoy life.

1 It is important to believe in your own judgement.
2 People who do the same things every day are sensible.

You should change what you do from time to time. Make sure you <u>vary</u> your daily routine – even if it's just <u>simple</u> things like not having the same food for breakfast or choosing a different route when you leave home in the morning. Then when a bigger choice comes along it won't seem so frightening.

3 Prepare for larger changes in your life by changing the small things you do.
4 Don't have breakfast some mornings to have more time to make decisions.

Doing something <u>physical</u>, such as going for a run or washing the dishes, allows your mind to run free. And you shouldn't be afraid to think while you're doing those everyday things. Apparently, Albert Einstein had some of his best ideas when shaving!

5 Doing the housework stops you from having useful thoughts.
6 Taking exercise provides important opportunities to use your brain.

Listening to your body is <u>essential</u> in all of this. Your body always says yes or no when you're about to make a decision. When it's a decision that's good for you, you'll develop a feeling of <u>calm</u>. If you make a <u>poor</u> decision, on the other hand, you'll probably get a stomachache or find it difficult to breathe.

7 You need to listen to the advice of others.
8 Poor decisions often make a person feel unwell.

Try this training exercise. Sit or lie down in a comfortable position. Take a deep breath. Feel yourself relax into the floor or chair. Take another deep breath and ask your body, 'What would you like to tell me?' As you breathe in and out, notice any positive or negative feelings you have, any pains or <u>worries</u> – and above all, listen! Your body may be trying to give you some useful information.

9 The training exercise described will help you to fall asleep.
10 The exercise will allow you to understand your body better.

7 Which of the words below are uncountable? Use some of them in sentences 1–5.

→ **GRAMMAR REFERENCE** PAGE 126

advice bit calm choice diary furniture game luggage money piece rubbish traffic

1 I'd like some .... about changing my bank account.
2 Have you got any .... with you? I'd like to buy a drink.
3 What you're saying is absolute .... !
4 When there's no .... in this room, it looks much bigger.
5 There isn't much .... on this road after seven o'clock.

EXAM TIP Remember that you cannot add -s to uncountable nouns.

Writing

8 The checklist contains things to remember when checking your sentences are properly formed. Read it and make any necessary corrections to the story.

- Does each sentence include a verb?
- Is there a subject in each sentence?
- Is the verb in the right tense?
- Is there a pronoun where necessary? Is the pronoun necessary?
- Is the word order in each sentence correct?

WAKE-UP CALL

[1]Jack he finds it difficult to get up in the morning. [2]His alarm clock every day at seven o'clock. [3]One morning two of Jack's friends called round, so that could walk to college together. [4]They knock on his door but they couldn't wake him up. [5]They borrowed from a neighbour a ladder. [6]They put against the wall. [7]One of Jack's friends climbed up and shouted through the window. [8]An angry old woman with blue hair she appeared. [9]It Jack's grandmother who sleeping in his room!

Warm up

1 The people in the photos have all taken some time off from their singing careers. Do you know why? Choose from 1–5.

1 to write a book
2 to relax
3 to have children
4 to recover from a breakdown
5 to act in films

2 Would you like to try something different? If so, what, when and why?

Listening

3 You will hear Jan's story on a radio programme. Before you listen, read questions 1–6 and underline the key words.

1 <u>Why</u> did <u>Jan</u> decide <u>not</u> to <u>accept</u> the <u>new job</u> on the <u>newspaper</u>?
2 What was the main disadvantage of Robbie's house?
3 Why did Jan feel that moving would be good for her?
4 What problems did Jan have when she first moved?
5 What did Jan realise during her friends' visit?
6 How does Jan manage to earn money now?

EXAM TIP When you listen to a long recording, it is sometimes difficult to follow so prepare yourself for what you will hear.

4 Listen and answer questions 1–6. The part that includes the answer is repeated.

Listen to the whole recording again and check your answers.

Grammar

Past simple and past continuous

➔ **GRAMMAR REFERENCE** PAGE 126

5 Match sentences 1–3 to a–c.

1 Four years ago, I was living in Manchester.
2 The paper offered me a different job.
3 I was planning to say 'yes', when my friend Robbie McPherson phoned.

a the past simple tense
b the past continuous tense
c both of these tenses

6 Read the sentences and complete the rules about past tenses with *past simple* or *past continuous*.

I decided to invite some friends from Manchester and we had a great time.
We use the .... to talk about events in the past or situations over a definite period of time.

I was working as a journalist on a local newspaper there.
We use the .... to talk about temporary situations in the past.

I was reading in the cottage when suddenly all the lights went out.
We also use the .... to talk about a situation in the past that is interrupted by an action or event. The verb connected with this action or event is in the .... tense.

7 Make sentences from prompts in A and B in which something is interrupted. Add any necessary words.

Example
I was cooking a meal when there was a power cut.

A	B
cook a meal	my mobile phone / ring
paint the ceiling	be / a power cut
try on a dress	hear / the news
play tennis	my friends / call round
study in the library	fall off / the ladder
travel in India	start to rain
write an essay	the zip / break

when

8 Complete the text by putting the verbs into the past simple or past continuous.

A Japanese penfriend

Last October, I *went* (go) to Japan for the first time, to visit my penfriend Misa and her family. Misa and I **1** .... (start) emailing each other three years ago, thanks to my geography teacher, Mr Brown. He **2** .... (set up) a link with a Japanese school because we **3** .... (learn) about Japan in our classes that term. Mr Brown **4** .... (feel) that we would find out more about the country if we **5** .... (have) contact with Japanese people and he **6** .... (be) right.

In our first few weeks of exchanging emails, Misa **7** .... (tell) me lots of interesting things about Japan. She also **8** .... (explain) where she **9** .... (live) and each week, **10** .... (describe) what she **11** .... (do) at school. Mr Brown also **12** .... (persuade) the language department to run Japanese classes after school. We really **13** .... (enjoy) learning Japanese and when other students at our school **14** .... (hear) how much fun we **15** .... (have), they **16** .... (ask) to join the class.

When our headteacher **17** .... (realise) that Japanese **18** .... (become) more and more popular in her school she **19** .... (suggest) developing a full exchange programme with the school in Japan. That's how I finally **20** .... (get) the chance to go to Japan and meet Misa.

Vocabulary

9 Complete sentences 1–6 with phrasal verbs formed with *get* and *give* and the particles below.

back   down   in   off
out   up

Example
Please *get down* from that ladder at once, before you fall.

1 What's the best way to .... smoking?
2 If you can't .... through the main gate, come round to the side entrance.
3 I'd like someone to .... these books – there's one for everyone in the class.
4 To get to my house you need to take the bus from the station and .... at the bottom of the hill.
5 What time do you usually .... in the morning?
6 Why don't you borrow the video over the weekend – you can .... it .... to me on Monday.

Speaking

10 Imagine you are famous. Discuss the questions.

- How would your life be different?
- What would you like and dislike about your new life?
- What would you miss from your old life?

Example
I wouldn't get up early in the morning any more.

Speaking

1 Look at the photos.

- What type of people would buy each camera?
- Which three types of advertising would you use to advertise them? Why?
  TV (which channels?)
  newspapers (which ones?)
  magazines (which ones?)
  posters (where?)
  public transport (which type?)
  on-line adverts (linked to which website?)
  leaflets (to whom?)

1

2

Vocabulary

2 Underline the adjectives and adverbs in the advert and write them in the table with the words they give more information about.

> **Introducing** *a stylish new palmtop with TV, internet, calendar, diary, bi-lingual dictionary and other special features.*
>
> → Check your email regularly wherever you are.
> → Set the alarm to remind you about meetings, appointments, etc. You can also choose how loudly the alarm rings.
> → Select a country and it will display the correct time.
> → Type in a foreign word and it immediately provides a translation. It also acts like a phrase book and quickly displays useful phrases for different situations.
> → Watch your favourite channel with a clear picture.
> → Fits neatly into your pocket!

Adjectives	Adverbs
stylish new (palmtop)	(check your email) regularly

3 Read the examples and complete the rules with *adjectives* or *adverbs*.

Toni bought a stylish new mobile phone.
It was perfect for sending text messages to her boyfriend.
We usually use .... before a noun in English, but .... which tell us about the quality of something, come after the verbs *be, seem, appear, look*.

The alarm went off noisily.
They spoke to him angrily.
We use .... to give information about how something happens, e.g. *quickly, calmly*, after the verb or after the object, if there is one.

4 Complete sentences 1–5 with the adjectives and adverbs.

carefully   cheap   complicated   different   difficult   expensive
perfectly   pleased   quietly   unfashionable

1 It's the most advanced laptop they make so it was very .... , but I'm very .... with it.
2 The video instructions were .... , but I read them .... and managed to get it working.
3 Melissa spoke so .... it was .... to hear her.
4 The shoes fitted .... , so Nicki bought two pairs in .... colours.
5 Vic's flat is in a(n) .... part of town, that's why it was so ....

Reading

5 Read adverts A–E and answer the questions about each one.

1 Is it advertising a product, place or service?
   A *It's advertising a product, a very small TV and radio.*
2 Where might you see it?
   A *You might see it in a magazine, a newspaper or in an on-line advert.*
3 Who is it aimed at? Give as much detail as you can.
   A *It's aimed at men between 25 and 50, who are very keen on watching sport on TV.*
4 What is the message of the advertisement? Try to explain it in your own words.
   A *The message is, 'You can carry this TV/radio with you everywhere to keep up to date with your favourite sports events'.*

A **Don't miss the match!**
This tiny TV/radio will keep you in the picture.

B **UNDER 25?**

Don't pay more than you need for your car insurance.
Phone now.

C *The world's greatest adventure park*
* * * * * * * * * * * * * * * * * *
Excitement and fun beyond your imagination

D

THINK MORE CAREFULLY
ABOUT YOUR NEXT MOVE –
PROFESSIONAL ADVICE ON WRITING THE BEST CV.

E It's quieter than a mouse, **but more powerful than a lion.**

Grammar

Comparisons

→ **GRAMMAR REFERENCE** PAGE 127

6 Underline the words used to make comparisons in the adverts in **5**.

7 Complete sentences 1–5 with these words and an appropriate form of the adjective or adverb given.

more   as … as   than   not as … as   less

1 I really enjoyed that author's first novel, but his second was .... – quite disappointing in fact. (interesting)
2 My new camera is much easier to carry. It's .... my old one. (heavy)
3 I can't understand what you are saying. Can you speak .... please? (slowly)
4 They've increased their prices by 10%, so this year's holidays are more .... last year's. (expensive)
5 Let us repair your watch – it will be .... new. (good)

8 Complete the second sentence of each pair using comparative adjectives and adverbs so that it means the same as the first. Read this information first.

- You can write between one and three words. Contracted forms, like *can't*, are two words.
- The meaning of the two sentences must be the same. Be careful with tenses.
- Your spelling must be correct.

Example
Shopping on the internet is quicker than supermarket shopping.
Supermarket shopping is *slower than* shopping on the internet.

1 My car insurance has cost a lot more this year than last year.
   My car insurance this year is not .... it was last year.
2 This alarm clock rings more loudly than all the other clocks we sell.
   This is .... alarm clock we sell.
3 The jeans are darker than they looked in the photo on the website.
   The photo on the website made the jeans look .... they really are.
4 The coffee maker didn't work as fast as the advert said.
   The coffee maker worked .... than the advert said.
5 Digital cameras are better than any traditional ones.
   Digitals cameras are .... cameras you can buy.

2.2 Are you a shopaholic?

Speaking

1 Listen to someone interviewing a shopper about his shopping habits. Tick the boxes and make notes of his answers in the table.

Shopping habits questionnaire

1 Which of these do you use for shopping?
   town centre ☐   out of town shopping centres ☐
   mail order ☐   TV shopping ☐   internet ☐

2 What time of day do you prefer to shop
   before 12 p.m. ☐   12–6 p.m. ☐   after 6 p.m. ☐

3 Which two of these do you spend most on?
   food & home ☐   clothes ☐   books ☐
   CDs & video ☐   children's items ☐

4 How much do you enjoy shopping?
   very much ☐   quite like it ☐
   not very much ☐   not at all ☐

5 What two improvements can you suggest for your town/area's shopping facilities?

   [   ]

6 Name

   [   ]

2 Work with a partner to ask and answer the shopping questionnaire.

Listening

3 You will hear a conversation about shopping habits. Listen and decide if sentences 1–4 are correct or incorrect.

1 The man took the first suit back to the shop.
2 The woman likes to choose all her own clothes.
3 The man only buys goods he wants.
4 The woman wore her new T-shirt to a party.

4 Listen again and decide who expresses opinions 1–5, the man or the woman.

1 People need to be sure about wanting something before they buy it.
2 The law allows me to take things back to the shop I bought them from.
3 Shop assistants believe customers are honest.
4 If shops charge high prices, they must expect people to bring things back.
5 It's fair to return goods if they are damaged.

5 Whose approach to shopping do you agree with, the man's or the woman's? Why?

Vocabulary

→ **VOCABULARY REFERENCE** PAGE 121

6 Complete sentences 1–9 with these words.

cash   charge   cost   discount   exchange
pay   price   receipt   return

1 How much did you .... for your new car?
2 How much is this suit? I can't see the .... on the ticket.
3 If I buy ten of these T-shirts, can you give me a .... because I want so many?
4 I don't have any .... on me at the moment. Can I pay by credit card?
5 If my friend has already got this book, can I .... it and get my money back?
6 How much do these videos .... ?
7 What did the shop .... you for repairing your computer?
8 I bought the wrong size T-shirt. Can I .... it for this one?
9 Always keep the .... for anything you buy, in case there's a problem with it.

7 Match the verbs to the correct picture 1–6.

fit   go with   put on   take off   try on   wear out

1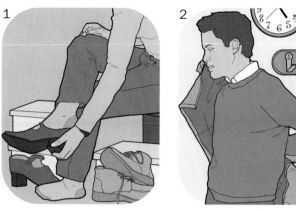

2

3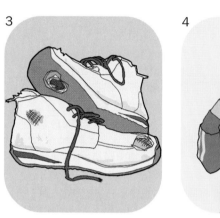

4

5

6

8 Complete sentences 1–6 with the verbs in **7** in the correct tense.

1 Excuse me, where are the changing rooms? I'd like to .... this ....

2 I've only had this jumper for a month, and it .... already .... at the elbows.

3 Does this top .... these trousers? I'm not sure about these colours together.

4 You'd better .... a coat this morning – it's really cold.

5 When she .... her jacket, I could see she was wearing her best dress underneath.

6 Do you think this .... OK? The sleeves are too long, aren't they?

Writing

9 Correct the punctuation in sentences 1–3.

1 where did you get your glasses. theyre very stylish,

....

2 i bought some new jeans. two tops. a hat and a new bag?

....

3 gina says she cant afford expensive clothes. but she buys new things all the time,

....

10 Where do we use capital letters in English? Choose from these categories.

☐ beginning of sentences

☐ people's names and titles

☐ countries, cities

☐ street names

☐ names of rivers, mountains, lakes

☐ titles of books, plays, newspapers

☐ days of the week

☐ months of the year

☐ seasons of the year

☐ nationalities

☐ festivals

☐ numbers

11 Add commas, full stops, capital letters and question marks to the short text.

> have you heard about the latest european shopping craze i was amazed to find out that some people shop just for excitement they don't want to buy anything but enjoy the feeling of trying on expensive clothes or buying something they don't need these people don't intend to keep their new things a few days later they take the goods back to the shops and expect to get their money back

3.1 Aches and pains

Vocabulary

➜ **VOCABULARY REFERENCE** PAGE 121

1 Look at the face and say which parts of it you think belong to which of the people in the list. Turn to page 108 if you need help.

Example

Whose nose is it?

I think it's Brad Pitt's nose.

1 Whose teeth, lips and gums are they?
2 Whose hair is it?
3 Whose chin and throat are they?
4 Whose eyes are they?

Brad Pitt

Gérard Depardieu

Kate Winslet

Robbie Williams

Catherine Zeta-Jones

Jennifer Aniston

David Beckham

Antonio Banderas

2 Divide the verbs into two groups, one connected to illness and the other with a return to health. Then complete sentences 1–5 with a suitable verb in the correct tense. More than one answer may be possible.

cure   get better   hurt   injure   recover   wound

1 Dave .... himself in the football match last Saturday.
2 Doctors are trying to find a new medicine to .... cancer.
3 Children often .... from illnesses more quickly than old people.
4 I hear you've been off sick all week. I hope you .... soon.
5 Six soldiers .... in a practice exercise at their army headquarters last month.

3 Match what each person says to pictures 1–3 and complete the sentences with the words.

breathe   cough   headache   sneezing   throat

Thomas – I've got a really bad cold. I can't stop .... and I can't concentrate because I've got a ....

Polly – I feel so ill. My body aches and it hurts when I ....

James – I don't feel very well at all. I've got a sore .... and I didn't sleep much last night because I couldn't .... through my nose. I'm sure I've got a temperature as well.

1

2

3

Listening

4 You will hear two people talking about their health problems. Listen and circle each thing in the pictures in 1 and 2 that is mentioned.

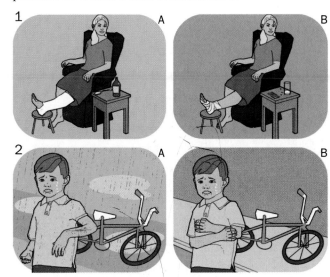

5 Listen again and decide which picture best shows the situation in the recording. Explain why you made your choice.

6 You will hear another three people talking about their health problems. Look at the pictures in 1–3. Before you listen, say what places they show. What things can you name in the pictures?

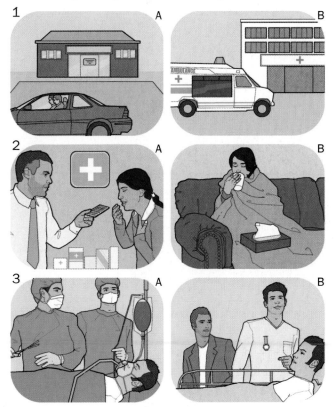

7 Listen and decide which picture best shows each situation. Explain why you made your choices.

Grammar

Ability and possibility

→ **GRAMMAR REFERENCE** PAGE 128

8 Read the dialogue. Do the underlined phrases express ability or possibility?

DOCTOR VINCENT Hello. I'm Doctor Vincent. I understand you've hurt your ankle. How did you do that?

PAULA I had a dance lesson last night and I fell down when I was practising. I think <u>it might be broken</u> – it's very painful.

DOCTOR VINCENT OK. Let's have a look. <u>Can you move your foot</u> up towards me? Good, and down to the floor? OK. And <u>can you stand</u>?

PAULA Ow, no, <u>I can't</u>. It hurts a lot. I <u>can move my toes</u> though. Do you think it is broken?

DOCTOR VINCENT Well, <u>it may be fine</u>, but I'm going to send you for an X-ray. <u>A small bone could be broken</u>. I'll get a wheelchair, as <u>you're not able to walk very well</u>.

9 Complete the rules about ability and possibility with *can*, *could*, *may*, *might* and *be able to*.

- We use .... , ... and .... to talk about possibility.
- We use .... and .... to talk about ability.
- Unlike other verbs, we do not put -s after the verb form for ....
- After *may*, *might*, *can* and *could*, we use other verbs without ....
- After the verb .... , we use verbs with *to*.
- We do not use an auxiliary verb to make questions with .... , ... , ... and ....

10 Correct sentences 1–6. Then decide which are about ability and which are about possibility.

1 Monica can't to move her arm.
2 She isn't able use her right hand at all.
3 Her mother thinks it mights be broken.
4 'Do you can lift your arm?' the doctor asked.
5 'No, I'm not able lift or turn it,' she replied.
6 'You might to need an x-ray' he said.

11 Choose the correct verb in 1–5.

Mia's not feeling very well. She thinks she **1** *might/can* have flu. She **2** *is able to/may* have a temperature. 'I've got a sore throat and I **3** *can't/mightn't* breathe properly – I keep sneezing. I think I'll go home,' she told the teacher. '**4** *Might/Can* you read and write?' he asked. ' Yes, of course,' Mia replied. 'Well, you **5** *might/are able to* do the exam this afternoon then,' he said.

3.2 Staying healthy

Warm up

1 Write down your answers to the questions.

- How often do you take exercise?
- In what ways is your diet healthy?
- In what ways is it unhealthy?
- Do you ever change your habits in order to be more healthy? What do you do?

2 Carry out a quick class survey by asking each other the questions. How does the class keep healthy?

Reading

3 Read the article. Which advice would improve *your* health?

Five ways to
good health

Look after your back

Back pain is very common, but there's a lot you can do to prevent problems occurring. Regular exercise will make your back stronger. Avoid soft sofas and mattresses. In the office make sure your chair is the right height for your desk and arrange your computer so that you can work comfortably.

Laugh

Believe it or not, laughing is good for your health! When you laugh, your brain produces a chemical which helps you fight off disease, and also makes pain easier to handle.

Avoid coffee

If you drink a lot of coffee, tea and cola you may experience a number of different health problems. You might often get headaches, you might not be able to sleep well and you might feel tired all the time. Try to find other drinks you enjoy – fruit tea or water, for example.

Wear sunglasses

Protecting your eyes from too much sunlight is essential for healthy eyesight. Experts say that wearing sunglasses helps to prevent typical eye problems we all experience as we get older.

Find out about your food

Read the packet before you buy something. It may say it's 80 per cent fat-free but that still means there's 20 per cent fat, which is high. 'No added sugar' doesn't mean that a product is sugar-free. Take the time to find out what you're eating, and ask yourself why you are buying something if it's really unhealthy.

4 Find words and phrases in the article which have a similar meaning to 1–6.

1 avoid
2 happening
3 illness
4 several
5 specialists
6 discover

5 Read the two descriptions and say how healthy you think these people are. Decide which of the 'Ways to good health' they should try. Why?

> Clara drives a delivery van. She doesn't eat much during the day, but there's always a can of cola in the van. In the evening, she heats a ready-made meal in the microwave.

> John is a journalist. He works at home, sitting at his computer all day. He goes for a quick run in the mornings before he starts work, and eats quite healthy meals.

6 Write a description like the ones for Clara and John about someone you know. Give it to your partner to say which two 'Ways to good health' would be best for that person.

Speaking

7 Your school or college is planning to have a Healthy Living week. With a partner say what healthy living ideas are shown in the photos. Then choose two ideas and talk together about their benefits and how you will persuade people to take them up.

Example
Doing yoga will make your body fitter and stronger. It's a good idea to take up yoga to help you relax.

Writing

8 Find eight mistakes with verb forms in the text and correct them.

DON'T CATCH A COLD THIS WINTER!

As winter approach, our bodies often becomes weaker, and we are more likely to get colds and flu.

DIET
Don't forget to keep eating a balanced diet. In the summer we generally eat more fresh fruit and vegetables and lots of salads. This kind of food are important all year round. An orange have many things in it which are good for us. It is also important to drink at least six glasses of water a day.

ACTIVITY
Your body need exercise regularly, even when it is cold and dark outside. There is plenty of different keep-fit activities – try to find one you like.

SLEEP
Sleep play an important role in our lives, by giving our bodies rest. If you doesn't get enough sleep, especially in the winter, you might become ill.

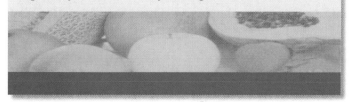

EXAM TIP It is important to check your writing for any mistakes.

4.1 Perfect homes

Warm up

1 Put the words into the correct group in the table. Some words can go into more than one group. Check you know what they all mean.

~~antique~~ armchair blanket carpet ceiling corridor courtyard curtain cushion duvet fan garage hall mirror passage pillow shed shower sofa stable stairs tap wardrobe

living room	bedroom	bathroom	all rooms	connecting rooms	outside
			antique		

Speaking

→ **VOCABULARY REFERENCE** PAGE 121

2 What do you like about where you live? Think about its *interior* (size / number of rooms, decoration and furniture) and its *exterior* (balcony / terrace / courtyard / garden and location).

3 In pairs, describe the people and the four homes A–D. Decide together which home would be best for each person. Explain why.

A
B

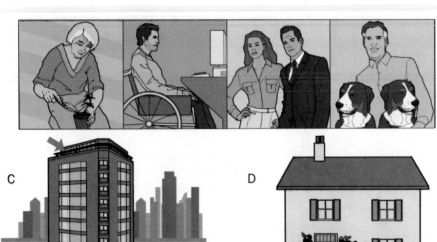

C
D

A Californian dream home

KELLY HARMON designs houses for people and their horses, although really, it's the opposite: she designs houses for horses and their people! Horses have been important to Kelly since she was a little girl and now they are part of her working life too. In Sullivan Canyon, Los Angeles, where film stars and millionaires go riding a few miles inland from the Pacific Ocean, she has designed her own perfect home.

The large, single-storey 1940s house is built around a courtyard. It was originally created by Cliff May, the favourite designer of many Hollywood stars. In May's ranch-style houses, the interior and exterior are <u>brought</u> together, in a design style close to Kelly's own heart. So, since buying the house twelve years ago with her

Reading

4 Read the first sentence of the article about Kelly Harmon, an American interior designer. What is special about the homes she designs?

5 Read the whole article to find out more about Kelly's home. Would you like to live in it? Why / Why not?

husband Robert, Kelly has redesigned it, adding a garage, her studio and, next to it, a stable for four horses. The studio and stable are connected by a stable door, which is a <u>typical</u> design touch of Kelly's – so a horse can join the family. All of this is on one <u>side</u> of the lavender-filled courtyard.

The family sleep in a separate part of the house, where both daughters' bedrooms <u>look</u> onto the garden. In addition, Kelly has created an unusual two-storey building for Robert and herself, connected by an open passage to the swimming pool. On the ground floor, their bedroom overlooks the terrace and there's a bathroom with a <u>deep</u>, oval bath – Kelly loves the shape because it's like something a horse would drink out of! Above the bedroom is Robert's office, which has two gorgeous leather armchairs the colour of baseball gloves.

The wooden ceiling of the living room is decorated with a beautiful blue-grey and stone-white pattern. Kelly has replaced the doors here with wonderful eighteenth-century French doors, which she found locally. But though the house appears to be total luxury, more than anything, Kelly sees it as a home – full of cats, dogs, horses and children. She says she is trying to create what is missing in modern American homes: a hand-made, hands-on, simpler style of living. And although Cliff May might not recognise his house at first glance, he would certainly approve of it. ■

6 Answer questions 1–6 to check your understanding.

1 What did Kelly like about Cliff May's way of designing houses?
2 Where is Kelly's studio?
3 Why do you think Kelly grows lavender in the courtyard?
4 Which room in the house is on the second floor?
5 What change has Kelly made to the living room?
6 According to the writer, how would Cliff May feel about Kelly's changes to the house?

EXAM TIP Remember that in Reading Part 5, A–D are the same part of speech within each question.

7 Look at the underlined words in the text. Decide what part of speech each one is – *adjective, adverb, noun* or *verb* – and use them to complete sets 1–5.

1 A watch   B see   C ....   D glance
2 A ....   B limit   C edge   D place
3 A high   B ....   C broad   D wide
4 A fetched   B taken   C carried   D ....
5 A normal   B central   C ....   D classical

Vocabulary

8 Find four adjectives in these examples that give the writer's opinion. Where do they appear in each phrase?

the large, single-storey 1940s house
an unusual two-storey building
a deep, oval bath
two gorgeous leather armchairs
a beautiful blue-grey and stone-white pattern
wonderful eighteenth-century French doors
modern American homes

9 The thirteen remaining adjectives all give descriptive information about the noun. Match each one to the six types of adjective in the table.

size	shape	age	colour	nationality	material
large					

10 Read the rule and check sentences 1–6. Reorder the adjectives if necessary.

Where there is more than one descriptive adjective, the adjectives follow the order in the table.

1 I swam in an amazing oval large swimming pool.
2 There were three leather Italian beautiful sofas in the room.
3 The kitchen had a horrible old wooden floor.
4 Sam bought two reddish-brown Moroccan ancient carpets.
5 The bath had a pair of unusual gold taps.
6 We walked through a mysterious nineteenth-century narrow passage.

11 Write five sentences about things in your home. Include opinion and descriptive adjectives.

4.2 Home from home

Warm up

1 The families who live in these houses have agreed to exchange homes for a fortnight for a holiday. How will each family benefit? What do you think they will each miss about their own home? Why?

2 Would you ever consider exchanging homes like this? Why / Why not? What could go wrong?

Writing

3 Read the messages and decide what order they were written in.

1

Dear Juan and Anita
Welcome! Hope you had a good flight? Our neighbour Roz (Grant) in the flat opposite has a spare key if you ever need it. Have a great time in the city. And don't worry, we'll look after your apartment!
Love Lisa and John

2

☎ Telephone message

Lisa
Bilbao's definite! Juan called back – the July dates you suggested yesterday are fine. Wow! Very exciting.
See you later, John

3

The Sharehomes agency has given me your name and address – we're hoping to exchange homes with someone in Spain. If you're planning an exchange in July and you're interested in staying in this part of London (see picture on the other side), let us know! You can email us on lisajohns@turquoise.com.
Best wishes
Lisa and John Smart

4

Important! One final thing, don't forget to set burglar alarm when you go out. Book of instructions on desk. Bye, Lisa

5

Outlook Express

From: juanm@spanie.es
To: lisajohns@turquoise.com

Yes, we'd really love to stay in your home. Do you have a house or a flat? Here in Bilbao, we have a beautiful apartment, quite near the sea. You'd love it. Well, phone me on 094 56 78 21 to discuss our plans.

4 Find the examples of informal language in the messages.

  1 contracted verb forms
  2 phrasal verbs
  3 notes and missing words
  4 single-word exclamations

5 Rewrite sentences 1–6 by using contracted forms and adding the words in brackets.

  1 I would like to visit you next month. (*really*)
  2 I have found out more about your city. (*lots / amazing*)
  3 I am keen to see the Guggenheim Museum. (*really*)
  4 Here is my chance! (*Well, finally*)
  5 I have heard that it is fantastic. (*absolutely*)
  6 I am looking forward to seeing you soon. (*very*)

6 Write a short message to a friend who is coming to visit you for the first time, giving basic details about where you live (35–45 words).

EXAM TIP In Writing Part 2 messages you will need to use informal language.

Listening

7 You will hear four answerphone messages. Listen and fill in the missing information for 1–4.

PHONE MESSAGES

Richard: I've just picked up Saturday's messages for you. Here they are:

1 Lisa Smart (going to Bilbao)
  Dates: .... July

2 Nicholas King (new customer) needs a catalogue. Address:
  .... Oxford OX3 9TF

3 Your sister, Sue, has invited you to lunch next Sunday .... at 12.45p.m. Call her on Monday.

4 John McTaggart (back from exchange in New York – house in a mess!) Phone his mobile number: ....

See you on Monday, Jill

Grammar

Imperatives

→ **GRAMMAR REFERENCE** PAGE 128

8 Tips 1–3 are taken from a website about home exchanges and all include imperative forms. Underline the imperatives used and match each one to uses a–c.

1	Leaving pets at home? Remember to tell the people to feed them!
2	Be careful not to leave any valuable jewellery on display.
3	To speak to one of our advisors, dial 0845 692103 now.

  a giving advice
  b giving instructions
  c giving warnings

9 Rewrite sentences 1–4 using imperative forms. Start with the imperative each time.

  1 You shouldn't play loud music late at night.
  2 The garden steps are steep, so care is needed.
  3 If there's a problem, it's best to contact the owners immediately.
  4 You mustn't leave the property in a mess.

Grammar

1 Choose the correct option for 1–10.

1 I .... when I heard a loud noise downstairs.
   A was falling asleep B fell asleep

2 When I lived in Manchester, I .... to the cinema twice a week.
   A was going B went

3 The new flats near us are .... expensive than the ones they're building in the centre of town.
   A more B the most

4 My grandmother is .... driver I know. She really shouldn't drive any more.
   A the least B the worst

5 .... to drive again, now you've recovered from your operation?
   A Can you B Are you able

6 CUSTOMER Have you got this T-shirt in light blue?
   SALES ASSISTANT We .... have it – I'll have a look for you.
   A might B can

7 Special offer – .... nothing until next year!
   A pay B paying

8 If you have an appointment, please .... straight to the patients' waiting room.
   A go B to go

9 I was buying a present for a friend, when I .... her in the same shop.
   A was seeing B saw

10 Children's diets are not .... they used to be.
   A as healthy as B less healthy than

2 Choose the correct word or phrase for 1–10.

Building your own house

Luke and Jane **1** *wanted / were wanting* a dream home. They liked old cottages, but needed a house with **2** *bigger / more big* rooms than a cottage, because they have a lot of furniture. The **3** *most / more* important thing was to have a dining room with a round table for twelve people because they really like cooking and often have friends round.

While they **4** *built / were building* it, they **5** *experienced / were experiencing* many different problems. They even had to knock it down and start again after a neighbour complained that he **6** *couldn't / mightn't* see the view over the countryside any more.

The finished house, however, is amazing. There is a bathroom on the first floor which is **7** *as big than / as big as* the perfect dining room below. From this room, the twelve guests **8** *are able to / might* enjoy the beautiful view. So what do Luke and Jane think now? They **9** *could / may* not tell me, because just after it was finished, they **10** *were moving / moved* to America. The family who rent it say it's wonderful!

Vocabulary

3 Number the adjectives in sentences 1–6 in the correct order.

1 The first model in the fashion show wore a *green, woollen, bright* dress.
2 Dave's living room is full of *old, beautiful, Turkish* carpets
3 You get to the house from a *dark, small* courtyard, up some *broken, stone* steps, but once you're inside, it's light and large.
4 The *Japanese, modern, small, best* music systems are half price in a sale at Kent's Department Store.
5 My cat always sleeps on my *pink, favourite, bright, cotton* blanket and leaves it covered in black hairs.
6 Kirsty's just bought an *antique, Swedish, unusual* mirror.

4 Complete sentences 1–6 with phrasal verbs with *get* or *give*.

1 It felt wonderful to .... the walking sticks to the clinic once my leg was better.
2 You don't have to take my advice – but I think you should .... running. It's damaging your knees.
3 By the time he got to the hospital Bill said he felt much better and .... of the ambulance without help.
4 I can't believe Charlie tried to .... the train while it was still moving!
5 '.............. from that wall before you fall off and hurt yourself!'
6 I couldn't .... this morning – my head ached and I had a terrible sore throat.

5 Choose the correct option for 1–8.

1 What do you do to check that clothes fit you?
  A wear them out   B try them on   C take them off
2 Which of these is **not** connected to getting your money back?
  A receipt   B return   C discount
3 Which of these is **not** part of a shirt?
  A a tie   B a collar   C a sleeve
4 Which of these is **not** part of your mouth?
  A your lip   B your tongue   C your thumb
5 Which of these is **not** inside your body?
  A your heart   B your chin   C your lungs
6 Which of these can you break?
  A a bone   B your gum   C your blood
7 In which of these could you keep a horse?
  A a shed   B a garage   C a stable
8 Which of these can you **not** walk through?
  A a corridor   B a ceiling   C a passage

Writing

6 Correct any errors in punctuation, capital letters, pronouns and verb forms in messages 1–3.

1

Dear Mum and Dad
How are you both. Im in paris
for a few days. kenzo have to
do some work over here, so
Ive come with he. the weathers
brilliant and the river seine
look beautiful. kenzo finish
early this afternoon, so were
going on a boat trip.

Love Beth

2

John
Marie need to see dr
Bastable this evening
because shes injured his
leg playing tennis. is
you able to take her. the
appointment it is at
6.05.
Helen

3

Hi Sam,
I'm glad youre enjoying the holidays. I'm not? its really boring here at home. mum
leave for work at 8.30 and my little brothers at school all day, so the flat seem
really quiet. i cant wait to go back to university next week. See you then,
Erica

7 Make this paragraph about a room more interesting by adding these adjectives.

comfortable enormous fresh greenish-blue huge leather low
single-storey sunny wonderful wooden

INSIDE THE
BEACH HOUSE

From the outside, it doesn't look special, just a small house above the beach. But when you go inside, you find a living room at least ten metres wide and almost as long. There are two sofas and on the table between them, there are always flowers. You can hear the waves hitting the beach below and the windows look straight out onto the ocean.

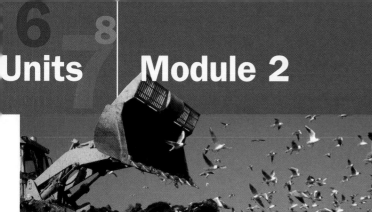

EXAM TASKS IN MODULE 2

Unit 5 – Paper 1 Writing Part 3 (letter)
Unit 6 – Paper 1 Writing Part 2
Unit 7 – Paper 1 Writing Part 3 (story)
Unit 8 – Paper 1 Writing Part 1

Make sure you read the relevant parts of the Exam guide before doing these tasks.

Topics

1 What is happening in the photos? What topics do they show?

Vocabulary

2 Find the odd word out in groups 1–4 and put it in the correct group. Then match groups 1–4 to the topics in **1** and add any more words you know.

1 bowl, fried, juice, knife, rain, roasted, vegetarian
2 bat, brick, championship, exercise, goal, run, track
3 apartment, cinema, dish, hotel, stadium, steel, theatre
4 air, cloudy, fog, pollution, thunder, trainer, windy

Grammar

3 Match sentences 1–4 to a grammar area a–d and underline the word(s) that show you this.

1 I often have cheese for breakfast.

2 Paolo doesn't study unless he has to.

3 Smoking is not allowed in this gallery.

4 Alex has bought a house.

a a perfect tense   c an adverb of frequency
b a passive   d a conditional sentence

5.1 Waste not, want not

The Remarkable Recycled Pencil™ is made from one recycled plastic drinks machine cup, yet it writes like a traditional pencil. The Remarkable Mousemat™ is made from recycled tyres which provide a fantastic non-slip surface for your mouse.

Warm up

1 What is unusual about the two products?

2 How many other everyday things can you think of which can be reused or recycled?

Reading

3 Read the text quickly and answer the questions. What is the topic of the text? Where would you read it?

4 Before you answer this question, read options A–D, underline the key words and find parts of the text which refer to them.

What is the writer's main aim in writing the text?
A to ask readers to give points to the school
B to encourage readers to join the recycling programme
C to warn readers about the health problems connected to mobile phones
D to tell readers to throw away their printer cartridges

5 Look closely at the meaning of those parts of the text you found and choose the best answer to the question in **4**.

Local school plans to turn trash into cash

INDIVIDUALS and companies in Swinford are being encouraged to save office materials that normally go into the rubbish bin, for example printer cartridges and old mobile phones, in order to help raise money for Swinford High School.

The school is working with a recycling company, Eurosource, in an exciting new programme to help the school get more equipment.

Every time someone gives in a used printer cartridge or old mobile phone, the school will receive a number of points. These will be exchanged for equipment the school chooses from a list.

Head Teacher, Mrs Sandra Kennedy, says 'Throwing away an old mobile phone or printer cartridge is not good for the environment. Mobiles contain a dangerous material which gets into the soil if phones are thrown onto rubbish sites.'

'Only five per cent of printer cartridges are recycled. The rest are buried in huge rubbish sites. Reports suggest that in the last ten years printer cartridges worth around £500m were thrown away. They can be cleaned, refilled with ink and used again. So, with this programme, we can help our students and the environment at the same time.'

Readers are asked to collect unwanted mobile phones, phone batteries and used printer cartridges from friends, relatives and neighbours, and from their workplace. They can be taken to the school between 8.45a.m. and 3.15p.m., or left at Wilson's Supermarket or Swinford Library. This is a great project for our local community and we encourage our readers to support it fully.

Grammar

The passive

→ **GRAMMAR REFERENCE** PAGE 128

6 Read the examples and complete the rules.

The Remarkable Company makes (pens) from old plastic bottles. (active)
(Pens) are made from old plastic bottles. (passive)

- The object of the .... sentence (pens) becomes the subject of the .... sentence.

- The verb in the passive sentence is in the same .... as in the active sentence (present simple).

- We use the .... when the action is more important than who does the action.

7 Complete the table with examples of the passive from the text in **3**.

what	verb *be*	tense of *be*	main verb – past participle
individuals and companies	are being	(present continuous)	encouraged

8 Make sentences in the passive using the prompts in 1–5.

Example

Students at Swinford High School / give / information about the recycling programme *past simple*

Students at Swinford High School were given information about the recycling programme.

1 The Remarkable Pencil / make / from one plastic cup *present simple*
2 3.5 million plastic cups / throw away / last year in Britain *past simple*
3 More recycled products / sell / in the future *future with will*
4 More than 80 million food and drinks cans / bury / in rubbish sites every day last year *past simple*
5 Old tyres / use / to make Remarkable Mousemats *present simple*

Vocabulary

→ **VOCABULARY REFERENCE** PAGE 122

9 Read the examples and complete the rules with *verb, noun* or *adjective*. Then put *re-* or *non-* in front of the words below to complete sentences 1–6.

Shoppers are encouraged to reuse plastic shopping bags.
The Mousemat provides a fantastic non-slip surface.
Support for new recycling plan was non-existent.
The idea of asking people to cycle to work was a non-starter.

Re- in front of a .... means *again*.
Non- in front of a ...., a .... or an .... means *not*.

essential   build   smoker   arrange   fill   returnable

1 I've got to work on Friday evening, so I can't come to the cinema any more. Can we .... it?
2 I hope everyone's a .... here. I'm afraid smoking isn't allowed anywhere in the building.
3 The house was very badly damaged by the fire, so they will have to .... it.
4 Don't buy drinks in those bottles. You can't recycle them because they are ....
5 They collect old printer cartridges and .... them with new ink.
6 Put all the .... equipment over there. We'll only take it if there's room in the car.

Speaking

10 Match the words and phrases to photos 1–3. Some can go with more than one photo.

air   atmosphere   beach
damage   dangerous gases
fish   glass   industry
large factories
last hundreds of years   oil
plastic bags   pollution
rubbish site   sea birds   spill
waste   wildlife

11 Use the words and phrases in **10** to talk about what dangers to the environment the photos show. Decide which photo shows the worst problem for the environment and say why.

Giving an opinion and reasons

I think … because …
… is the worst problem because …
In my opinion …

5.2 What's it like there?

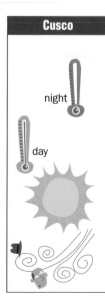

Warm up

1 Look at the photos. Describe what you can see and say what you think the climate is like in these places.

Vocabulary

→ **VOCABULARY REFERENCE** PAGE 122

2 Think about a place you have visited. Make a list of nouns you associate with that place using these to help and any of your own.

beach   cliff   desert   field   forest   harbour   hill
lake   mountain   river   sand   sea   valley

Example

French Alps in winter

mountains, snow, ice, trees, ski lifts

3 Describe the place you chose to your partner and say whether you liked it and why.

4 Choose the correct word or phrase in sentences 1–8.

1 It was *very windy / a strong wind* in Chicago yesterday.
2 It was *a fog / foggy* all day in Manchester.
3 It *rained / rainy* for three days last week.
4 It *snowy / snowed* in the north of the country overnight.
5 There was *a fog / fog* in Moscow yesterday.
6 In London there was *windy / a strong wind* all afternoon.
7 There were *storms / stormy* for most of our visit.
8 It is often *clouds / cloudy* and grey in London.

5 Imagine you are going on holiday to Peru. The holiday company has sent you notes about the weather in August. In pairs, take it in turns to describe what each place will be like.

Lima	Iquitos	Cusco

Listening

6 Listen and choose the correct picture in 1–5.

1 What will the weather be like tomorrow?

2 What was the weather like for most of the holiday?

3 Where did the girl go on holiday?

4 Where are they going to meet?

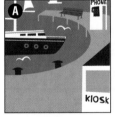  

5 Where were the woman's sunglasses?

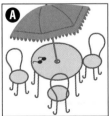 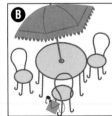 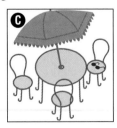

Writing Part 3 Letter

→ **EXAM GUIDE** PAGE 114

7 Read the task. What does it ask you to do?

- This is part of a letter you receive from an English penfriend.

> In your next letter, please tell me all about your favourite place. What's it like? Why do you enjoy going there?

- Now write a letter answering your penfriend's questions.
- Write your letter in about 100 words.

8 Read the letter from Dan answering the task in **7**. What information does Dan give about his favourite place? Make notes about points 1–4.

1 what you can see there
2 what you can do there
3 the weather
4 why Dan enjoys going there

Dear Stefan

Thank you for your letter. I'm writing to tell you about the Denali National Park in Alaska in the USA. It's a very beautiful place. There are mountains covered with snow all year round. A lot of the land is forest and there are a lot of lakes and islands. Bears are common and they often fish in the rivers and streams, and in the waterfalls, too.

The weather is often cold and rainy. But in the summer there's no sunset. It's light 24 hours a day. I visited the park to go fishing, to see the wildlife and to enjoy the amazing scenery. It's the best place I've ever been. I think you'd like it.

Best wishes

Dan

9 Write your own answer to the task in **7**.

EXAM TIP In Writing Part 3 remember to include *Dear ...* at the beginning of every letter and add a suitable ending, such as *With love, Take care, See you soon.*

6.1 Go for gold!

Warm up

1 Discuss the questions.
- Which world sports competitions do photos 1 and 2 represent?
- What do you know about the competitions?
- What big sports competitions are there in your country?

Choose two and write three facts about each one.

2 Make a list of sports connected to the first photo.

Vocabulary

➡ **VOCABULARY REFERENCE** PAGE 122

3 Put the words into the correct part of the table.

~~ball~~ bat (n+v) boxer court cup draw game goal hit
jump kick lose match medal net pitch player pool
racket reserve (n) run runner sail (n+v) score (n+v)
stadium swimmer team track win winner

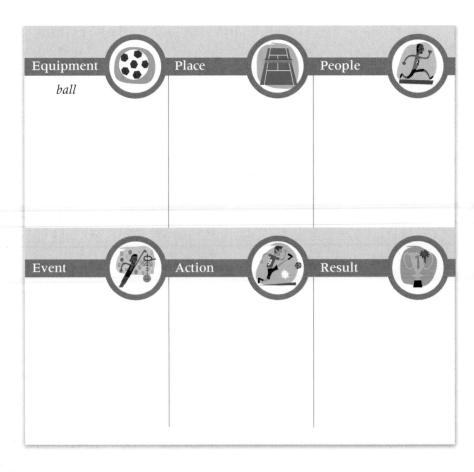

Equipment	Place	People
ball		

Event	Action	Result

4 Choose three of the sports you listed in **2**. How many of the words in the table can you match to each sport?

Listening

5 You will hear an interview with Dave Clamp, a successful sportsman. Listen to the first part of the recording to find out which sports he competes in.

6 Listen to the whole interview and answer questions 1–4.

1 In an Ironman event, how far do competitors run?
2 What did Dave do after the Paris marathon?
3 How does Dave handle the long distances involved?
4 How does Dave use his experience to help his students?

7 Turn to page 107. Choose the answer, A, B or C which is closest to your answer for each of the questions in **6**.

Grammar

Adverbs of frequency

→ **GRAMMAR REFERENCE** PAGE 129

8 Add the adverbs *rarely, regularly, hardly ever* and *usually* to the list in the correct places. Which two adverbs have similar meanings? Which adverbs can go in different places in a sentence?

always

often

sometimes

never

9 The adverbs in the sentences are in the wrong place. Rewrite sentences 1–5 correctly.

1 Germany lose hardly ever an international football match.
2 Ice hockey players wear protective clothes always.
3 Rarely England win a cricket match.
4 Footballers play sometimes golf to relax.
5 Never has Tim Henman won the Wimbledon Tennis Championship.

Present simple and present continuous

→ **GRAMMAR REFERENCE** PAGE 129

10 Underline and name the tenses in sentences 1–4. Then match 1–4 to the uses of the present tenses a–d.

1 Dave goes for a long run every weekend.
2 The triathlon involves swimming, cycling and running.
3 Dave is training for the world championship next year.
4 He's talking about his sports experiences in the radio studio.

a a regular activity
b something happening now
c a known fact
d something happening over a period of time

11 Complete the text about a famous cyclist by putting the verbs in the present simple or present continuous.

Lance Armstrong

Winning the Tour de France cycle race **1** .... (become) a habit for Lance Armstrong. For the fifth year running the US Postal Service rider **2** .... (be) the fastest rider in this three-week test. He has regularly won more than one stage of the race. These few facts **3** .... (tell) us a lot about the man who returned to racing in 1998 after winning a harder test – against cancer. It **4** .... (be) a story which people have often talked about over the past few years, but Lance **5** .... (insist) it has helped make him a Tour winner. 'Cancer has made me stronger,' he **6** .... (say).

Now the race is over, Lance **7** .... (relax) with his team mates and **8** .... (enjoy) some time off. The team **9** .... (be) very close and Lance **10** .... (know) how much they and the team director, Johan Bruyneel, **11** .... (support) him during his races. His victories, however, **12** .... (be) also due to the fact that he always prepares thoroughly for each event.

6.2 Sport for all

Reading

2 Find words and phrases in A which have a similar meaning to the words and phrases in B.

A
improve your skills
demanding
lively
sociable
anxious

B
active
practise
meet people
stressed
challenging

Speaking

1 Do the following in pairs.

- Each choose a photo and describe it.
- What do you remember about learning a new sport? Make notes about what you enjoyed and didn't enjoy about it. Then tell each other about your experiences.
- Talk together about the differences between team and individual sports. Which do you each prefer and why?

Classes at the Sports Centre

Table tennis

This is a sociable class where you can play as much or as little as you want to. Learn from our experienced players, enter mini-competitions, or unwind and play a game for fun, where it doesn't matter who wins.

All year – Mondays and Fridays 8–9.30p.m. £3 per class, no need to come every week.

Bodywork

Bodywork is a course which adds simple fun dance steps to traditional exercises to help you keep fit. The class ends with 10 minutes relaxing time. Suitable for anyone – you decide on your own goals.

30 weeks, £150, Tuesdays 6.30–7.30p.m.

Climbing

We have a new climbing wall at the Sports Centre! Come to our Open Day on Saturday 17th September. Experts will demonstrate how to move up the wall, and will help you to try it for yourself. Experience the challenge of working hard with your mind and body.

Half-day classes on Saturday afternoons, 1.30–5.30p.m., £10.

Squash

If you're stressed after a day's work, a fast game of squash will calm you down. Players develop their skills, learn how to plan their matches and study how other people play. Suitable for more advanced players. A competition is held each term.

10-week terms, £80 per term, Thursdays 7.30–9p.m.

Volleyball

Volleyball is a lively team sport which is becoming more popular in this country. We welcome beginners and more experienced players. We start with a few exercises, learn how to hit the ball and spend some time practising. Then we enjoy a friendly game.

10-week terms, £80 a term, Wednesdays, 7.30–8.30p.m.

3 Paul, Atsuko and Marcus all want to go to a class at the Sports Centre. Read what Paul says, then read the information sheet and find words and phrases which are connected to the underlined phrases.

I have a ¹difficult job and need to relax. I'd like to ²meet other people and ³enjoy a sport without having to enter competitions. ⁴I can't go regularly.

Example

1 *If you're stressed after a day's work* [squash], *calm down* [squash], *unwind* [table tennis]
2 *sociable* [table tennis]
3 ....
4 ....

> **EXAM TIP** In Reading Part 2 you need to look for words, phrases and parts of sentences which are connected by topic or have a similar meaning.

4 Read what Atsuko and Marcus say and find words and phrases in the information sheet which are connected to the underlined phrases.

I like to be ¹active. I want to ²play a sport with other people. I'm ³keen to improve, but ⁴don't want to play too seriously. My husband can baby-sit on Wednesday and Thursday evenings.

I'm very fit and ¹I'd like to learn some new skills. I like ²demanding activities where I need to ³concentrate hard and think carefully about what I'm doing. I work in the evenings at the end of the week.

5 Which class is best for each person? Use the words and phrases you matched in **3** and **4** to help, and think about when each person says they can go.

Writing Part 2

➜ **EXAM GUIDE** PAGE 113

6 Read the postcard. Tick the things Eva includes from the list below.

> Dear Kim
>
> I'm really enjoying learning about windsurfing. I've always liked water sports and this is a great challenge. Yesterday we had a professional demonstration before trying it ourselves. My favourite thing is the calm, blue sea. Don't forget our tennis match next Tuesday.
>
> Love Eva

1 says what sport she's doing ☐
2 suggests Kim tries windsurfing ☐
3 explains why she's taken it up ☐
4 apologises for not going to Kim's party ☐
5 thanks Kim for telling her about the sport ☐
6 tells Kim what she did the day before ☐
7 tells Kim what she likes best ☐
8 reminds Kim when they are meeting ☐

7 Look at the things in the list Eva doesn't include in her postcard. Which of these phrases could she use to start those sentences?

I'm sorry ...   Why don't ...?   Thanks for ...

8 Read the task and write an answer.

You are attending a sports event.
Write a postcard to your friend Stefan. In your postcard, you should

- explain what the event is
- say what you are enjoying most about it
- suggest Stefan could go with you next time.

Write 35–45 words.

> **EXAM TIP**   In Writing Part 2 remember to include information on all three points. For prompts starting with *explain*, *say* and *tell*, you will have to invent situations and events.

7.1 Body fuel

Warm up

1 Make a list of everything you have eaten and drunk since you got up this morning. Then decide which of these things are good for you and your body and which aren't.

2 What might the two people in the photos eat just before their races begin? What types of food would Ellen MacArthur need to eat on board during a race? Why?

Reading

3 Read the article quickly. What is Michael Schumacher's diet before and after a race?

4 Decide whether questions 1–5 are about someone's opinion or about the detailed meaning of the article. Then read the article carefully and mark the parts that give you the answers.

1 What does Degli Esposti think about his relationship with other Ferrari employees?
2 Why did Degli Esposti have problems when he started in the job?
3 What does Degli Esposti say about cooking in different locations?
4 Why do drivers need to follow a special diet before a race?
5 Why doesn't Michael Schumacher eat what everyone else eats before racing?

Ellen MacArthur, winner of 2002 Route du Rhum single-handed race

MEALS on WHEELS

As the drivers of Formula One complete their qualifying race to decide tomorrow's positions, a different race against time is happening near the track. In tiny kitchens, the Ferrari team cooks are busy preparing lunch. Head chef Claudio Degli Esposti loves his job: 'I get on very well with the whole team and they make me feel really part of things. You have the chance to travel all over the world. I don't see much of the racing,' he laughs, 'more of the kitchen! But there's a TV screen, so I know what's going on even when everyone's at the track.'

Unlike many Formula One kitchens, Degli Esposti's contains no tins or jars, because he only uses fresh food. He has a large fridge filled with cheeses, hams, sausages and fruit. 'In the beginning, it was very difficult, working in a small space without a lot of equipment. Now I know the places to shop near every track. I can get whatever I need, although things aren't equally good everywhere. For example, I love to cook fish, but unless it's absolutely fresh, I won't touch it.'

The drivers each have their own food plan, designed to prepare them for racing at high speed. The temperature inside the car is much hotter than outside, so during a race, drivers can lose a lot of water from their body, unless they have the right diet. Degli Esposti explains that Michael Schumacher's personal trainer prepares everything he eats before qualifying and racing. 'He usually has something very light, but when the race is over, he sits down and enjoys the same food as the rest of the team.'

5 Decide which questions in **4** fit each set of options A–D. Two questions are not used. Then choose the correct answers, explaining your choice.

A He would like to be better informed by them.
B It is stressful when they are travelling together.
C He feels involved with what the team is doing.
D Some team members are unhelpful in the kitchen.

A You cannot always find food of the same quality.
B It is sometimes necessary to hire equipment locally.
C You have to carry some tinned food with you.
D There aren't enough shops close to every track.

A So that they won't feel hungry out on the track.
B In order to concentrate on plans for the race.
C So that they can handle the heat while driving.
D In order to reduce their body weight in the car.

Michael Schumacher, Formula 1 racing driver

6 Would you like to have Claudio Degli Esposti's job? Why / Why not?

Grammar

Conditional clauses

→ **GRAMMAR REFERENCE** PAGE 130

7 Degli Esposti says that he won't buy fish if it isn't fresh. Find his exact words in the article. Which word does he use instead of *if …not*?

In conditional sentences, *if* can be followed by a negative or an affirmative verb form (for example, *isn't / is*). *Unless* means *if not*, so it cannot be followed by a negative verb.

8 Complete conditional sentences 1–8 with *if* or *unless*.

1 We won't be able to cook that chicken tonight .... you take it out of the freezer now.
2 .... they arrive within the next ten minutes, the meal will be overcooked.
3 Don't eat so much fried food .... you want to lose weight.
4 .... you buy mushrooms at the market, they're much cheaper – and fresher too.
5 That soft cheese will go off .... you keep it in the fridge.
6 I'm sure you'll love this fruit tart, especially .... you try it with ice-cream.
7 There isn't enough time to bake the potatoes .... we use the microwave.
8 .... you forget to add any salt, you can't expect vegetables to taste good.

9 Match 1–8 and a–h to make conditional sentences, joining them with *if* or *unless*.

1 These days, I won't buy beef or lamb
2 Don't open another tin of tomatoes
3 Marathon runners can't keep going
4 You have to check food labels carefully
5 You can't have any dessert
6 I stop and eat some chocolate
7 You'll need to buy more flour
8 It's hard to lose weight by dieting

a they drink water at regular intervals.
b I'm feeling tired on a long walk.
c you have a problem eating nuts.
d you want to bake a cake this afternoon.
e I know exactly where it's from.
f you take lots of exercise too.
g it's just a small one.
h you finish your vegetables!

7.2 Special recipes

1
2
3
4
5
6
7

Speaking

3 In pairs, each choose one of the photos. Make notes on what you could say about 1–3.

1 where the photo was taken
2 what seems to be happening
3 who appears in the photo

4 Talk about your photo using your notes. Add suggestions about your partner's photo.

5 Which job would be more tiring, a waiter's or a chef's? Would you like to have a job connected with food? Why / Why not?

Warm up

→ **VOCABULARY REFERENCE** PAGE 123

1 Can you name the ingredients in the photos? Describe how they taste, using these words to help you.

bitter   fishy   hot   rich
salty   sour   sweet

2 What are the ingredients of your favourite dish? How is it prepared?

Listening

6 You will hear a conversation between a young chef, Kelly, and her boyfriend, Dan. Before you listen, read sentences 1–6 below. Which are only about facts? Which include Kelly or Dan's attitudes or opinions?

1 Kelly was 18 years old last June.
2 Kelly's boss has encouraged her to enter the competition.
3 Dan and Kelly agree that a dessert containing oysters would taste horrible.
4 Dan is being serious when he tells Kelly she's good at cooking.
5 Dan thinks Kelly should concentrate on one future aim in the essay.
6 Kelly believes she has a good chance of winning the competition.

7 Listen and decide whether sentences 1–6 are correct or incorrect.

8 Listen again with the tapescript in front of you (page 107). Check your answers by underlining the relevant parts.

Vocabulary

9 Make phrases from the words in A and B.

A	B
a bowl of	cake
a cup of	coffee
a jug of	salt
a slice of	soup
a teaspoonful of	water

Writing Part 3 Story

→ **EXAM GUIDE** PAGE 114

10 Read the story and suggest a suitable title for it.

LAST SATURDAY, I went to a top seafood restaurant with my family for a special meal. Everything went wrong! First, they couldn't find our name in the bookings and gave us a tiny table in the corner. Next, they took ages to bring us the menu. Then, the waiter dropped a plate of spaghetti all over my little brother. He was very upset. Later, they brought us the wrong fish. Shortly after that, something furry ran across the room towards us. It was a rat, which brushed my foot as it ran under our table! My father shouted for the manager. Finally, we only had to pay for our drinks and had a wonderful pizza down the road.

EXAM TIP In Writing Part 3 Story you need to make the order of events clear. Use linking words to do this.

11 Underline six words or phrases in the story which order events. Then put sentences 1–6 in the order you would like this meal to be served in. Link them together using the words and phrases you underlined.

1 A lemon tart and three kinds of ice-cream appeared.
2 There was roast lamb with spinach and peas.
3 The waiters carried in a huge bowl of fish soup.
4 We were given a delicious wild mushroom risotto.
5 We helped ourselves to a mixed green salad.
6 They bought us a pot of fresh coffee and some chocolates.

12 Read the task and plan your story.

• Your English teacher has asked you to write a story.
• Your story must have this title:

A special celebration

▼ Think about what the celebration might be for and where it might take place.
▼ Write down the events you will include and some linking words that will order your ideas.
▼ Decide how you will end your story (perhaps you could say how you felt afterwards?)
▼ Write your story in about 100 words.

8.1 Old building, new use

BALTIC

1 BALTIC is a new international centre for contemporary art, which has just opened in the north of England. Situated on the south bank of the river Tyne in Gateshead, it lies right at the heart of Gateshead Quays, an important area of redevelopment on Tyneside.

Warm up

1 Is it better to protect old buildings or to knock them down and build new ones? Why? Is it sensible to add new buildings to old ones, as in the Louvre in Paris? Do you know of any old buildings that have changed their use?

Speaking

2 Your town wants to turn this empty building into a useful facility. What would you turn it into? Discuss all the ideas shown and decide on the best choice.

Reading

3 Read the text about BALTIC quickly and say what each numbered paragraph is about, choosing from a–e.

a the building's history
b what else is available
c BALTIC's location
d how the building looks now
e about the art there

> **EXAM TIP** In Reading Part 3 the sentences appear in the same order as the information in the text.

4 Read the text more carefully and underline the parts that cover the information in sentences 1–10. The first one has been done for you.

1 BALTIC's location is in the centre of Gateshead Quays.
2 There is no permanent collection at BALTIC.
3 Art will be specially prepared for display there.
4 The Baltic Flour Mills was an important employer.
5 Local people wanted the building to reopen.
6 Dominic Williams produced the prize-winning entry.
7 The new building contains a lot of glass.
8 The size of the art spaces can be changed.
9 It is possible to see a film at BALTIC.
10 Visitors can enjoy excellent views while eating a meal.

The centre doesn't own a single work of art – not one painting or drawing. Instead, it offers a new type of public art space, with a changing programme of exhibitions and events. For this reason, BALTIC's director Sune Nordgren considers it not an art gallery but an 'art factory', and will regularly invite artists to produce work for its exhibitions.

The building was originally part of a factory where flour was produced. Opened in 1950, the Baltic Flour Mills provided work for several hundred people and consisted of five buildings altogether. The factory was very successful until a serious fire in 1976 caused £500,000 worth of damage. It closed in 1982.

The building stood empty for many years, but people in Gateshead were keen to see it used again. In 1994, architect Dominic Williams won a competition to redesign the brick building as an art centre. BALTIC now has six storeys and its walls and roof are made of glass, to allow plenty of natural light in. Some interior walls are movable, which means that the art spaces within the building can easily be made bigger or smaller.

Apart from the actual art areas, the facilities offered include a cinema and lecture space, and a shop. There are three separate eating areas, including the wonderful Rooftop Restaurant, from which it is possible to see the cities of Gateshead and Newcastle.

Vocabulary

→ **VOCABULARY REFERENCE** PAGE 123

5 Read the examples. Then add -*ful* or -*able* to the nouns and verbs in 1–10.

The factory was very *successful*.
Some interior walls are *movable*.

1 If someone can afford a house, it is ....
2 If something is of value, it is ....
3 If you have hope for the future, you are .... about it.
4 If you enjoy something, you find it ....
5 If people help you, they are .... to you.
6 If a style is in fashion, it is ....
7 If something can be recycled, it is ....
8 If you accept something, you find it ....
9 If you doubt something, you are .... about it.
10 If something gives you pleasure, it is ....

Grammar

Present perfect

→ **GRAMMAR REFERENCE** PAGE 130

6 Match sentences 1–3 to the uses of the present perfect a–c.

1 The building has stood next to the Tyne for more than fifty years.
2 BALTIC has just opened.
3 The company has closed two of its factories.

a a recent event or action (How do you know?)
b something which started in the past and is still going on
c something which happened in the recent past but we don't know when

7 Complete sentences 1–5 by putting the verbs given into the present perfect and including the time adverbs. Use contracted forms.

Example
You *'ve already bought* (buy, already) the flat, haven't you?

1 The director .... (announce, just) that the theatre will close in May.
2 We .... (decide, already) to look for a two-bedroomed cottage on the coast.
3 The company .... (move, recently) to a bigger site.
4 I .... (like, never) Kevin's house – it's too dark.
5 The gallery .... (become, suddenly) much more popular since the new director arrived.

8 Ask and answer questions 1–5 using the present perfect and the time adverbs in brackets.

Example
visit London (ever) *Have you ever visited London?*
Yes, I went two years ago. It was very interesting.

1 make plans for this evening (already)
2 done anything dangerous (ever)
3 want to travel abroad (never)
4 win a prize (ever)
5 see a live band (recently)

8.2 State of the art

Reading

1 Do you know which country the building in the photo is in? What is it used for? When was it built?

2 Read the text. What is unusual about the building?

THE SAPPORO DOME

Grass doesn't grow without sunshine, **1** *what / which* means that you can't have grass in an indoor stadium. Or does it?

The Japanese city of Sapporo, **2** *which / whose* climate consists of snow for half the year, could never have an outdoor stadium. So for the 2002 World Cup, the organisers wanted to build an indoor stadium **3** *what / that* would be usable all the year round, but they had to provide a natural grass pitch for football.

The stadium they built, the Sapporo Dome, is in fact two separate areas. The indoor stadium, **4** *which / what* is covered by a round silver roof, is used mainly for baseball. Next to it, there is a second outdoor area, **5** *where / whose* a grass football pitch can be grown when the weather allows. To use the Dome for football, this pitch or 'hovering soccer stage', **6** *what / which* floats on a bed of air, is simply moved inside the stadium.

3 Choose the correct word in 1–6. What do the answers have in common?

→ GRAMMAR REFERENCE PAGE 130

4 Read the text again and answer 1–4.
1 Give as much information as you can about the weather in Sapporo.
2 Name two sports that can be seen in the Sapporo Dome.
3 Explain why the Dome has two playing areas.
4 Describe how the grass pitch is prepared for use.

Vocabulary

5 Complete sentences 1–6 with these verbs in the correct tense.

fall   hammer   nod   rock   sink   spill   wave

1 Fred .... the final nail into the wooden door frame.
2 The crying baby .... to sleep by his patient mother.
3 A huge amount of oil .... from the ship before it .... to the bottom of the sea.
4 The wind was so strong yesterday that several branches broke and .... to the ground.
5 Tom .... goodbye from the car as he drove away.
6 Helena .... her head to show she agreed with what he was saying.

Writing Part 1

→ **EXAM GUIDE** PAGE 112

6 Read the rules and complete the examples.

Words ending in *y* – the *y* changes to *i*
· in plural forms

story > ....
activity > ....

· in comparative and superlative forms

heavy > .... > *heaviest*

· in the present tense 3rd person singular verb form and past tenses

I study > *He* .... > *She studied*

Words that end 'consonant-vowel-consonant' double the final consonant when *-ed*, *-er*, *-est*, *-ing*, *-y* are added

rob > ...., *begin* > *beginner*

> **EXAM TIP**   In Writing Part 1 you must spell the answer correctly to get the mark.

7 Here are some sentences about building new houses.
For each question, complete the second sentence so that it means the same as the first.
Use no more than three words.

Example
Until now, new houses have been quite similar in design.
Until now, new houses haven't been very .... in design.

Answer: | 0 | *different* |

---

1 Nowadays, computers make it easy for architects to change their designs.

   It is .... than it was for architects to change their designs, because of computers.

2 This means that houses can be planned individually with their buyers.

   This means that architects can .... individually with their buyers.

3 For example, buyers can decide on the size of their rooms.

   For example, buyers can decide .... big their rooms should be.

4 If a room needs to be bigger, the architect can change the plan on screen.

   If a room isn't big .... , the architect can change the plan on screen.

5 Some architects argue that quality will suffer if they lose design control.

   Some architects argue that .... they keep design control, quality will suffer.

Listening

8 You will hear a woman talking on the radio about a competition for young architects, called EuroPan. Before you listen, decide which spaces (1–6) can be filled by a number, an adjective or a noun.

> EuroPan: competition for young architects
>
> Now offered in ¹........................... European countries.
> Examples of past themes:
>   1989 Lifestyles   2001 City ²...........................
> Someone from Holland won 1989 competition in ³........................... .
> Top prize in every country: ⁴........................... Euros.
> After each competition:
>   international catalogue published and
>   ⁵........................... exhibition organised
> Website written in ⁶........................... .

9 Listen and write in the missing numbers or words.

Speaking

➜ VOCABULARY REFERENCE PAGE 123

10 What will office buildings be like in 50 years' time? Discuss the questions.
   • Will they be tall or not? Why?
   • Will they be in the centre or outside the city? Why?
   • What materials will they be built in?
   • What will the spaces inside these buildings be like?

Grammar

1 Complete the second sentence of each pair so that it means the same as the first, using no more than three words.

1 Less energy is used to make things from recycled material.
Making things from recycled material .... energy.

2 I cook very little meat except at the weekends.
Apart from at the weekends, I .... ever cook meat.

3 George has always lived in fashionable areas of the city.
George has .... in unfashionable areas of the city.

4 Ten million mobile phones were thrown away in Britain last year.
Last year people in .... ten million mobile phones.

5 Don't enter a race if you haven't trained properly for it.
Don't enter a race .... have trained properly for it.

6 The leg of lamb is left in yoghurt for 24 hours and then roasted.
Before you roast the leg of lamb, you .... in yoghurt for 24 hours.

7 Students were asked to buy recycled paper to help save trees.
The college .... to buy recycled paper to help save trees.

8 The cottage is rentable all year and belongs to a Swedish writer.
The cottage, ... be rented all year, belongs to a Swedish writer.

9 Shoppers are encouraged to resuse plastic shopping bags.
Supermarkets .... to reuse plastic shopping bags.

10 Arsenal was beaten 2–1 last night by the French team Auxerre.
The French team Auxerre .... 2–1 last night.

2 Choose the correct adverb of frequency in 1–10.

Five a day

My daily diet **1** *always/often* includes at least five pieces of fruit – two bananas a day, an apple and whatever else is available. In winter, clementines are my favourite fruit but in summer, I **2** *never/regularly* enjoy a bowl of soft fruit like strawberries.

I **3** *rarely/usually* buy fruit from the local market because it's cheaper there, but **4** *hardly ever/sometimes*, I get fruit at the supermarket. They **5** *often/never* have special offers there: if you buy one bag of oranges, you get another free.

I grow some fruit in the garden, but I've **6** *regularly/never* tried to plant my own apple trees, as there isn't enough space. In June, there are **7** *usually/rarely* plenty of strawberries, which **8** *hardly ever/always* taste delicious freshly picked especially on a sunny day! Because the home-grown ones taste so much better, I **9** *hardly ever/sometimes* buy strawberries. They are **10** *regularly/rarely* as good.

Vocabulary

3 Choose the correct option for 1–10.

1 Where do you play tennis?
   A on a pitch   B on a court   C on a track

2 Who plays in a football team?
   A boxer   B runner   C goalkeeper

3 Which of these is **not** a watersport?
   A surfing   B sailing   C squash

4 Which is the smallest building?
   A cathedral   B cottage   C palace

5 Which of these is made of glass?
   A bottle   B can   C newspaper

6 How does food taste if you add sugar?
   A salty   B spicy   C sweet

7 What can you put on salad?
   A milk   B oil   C soup

8 Where are potatoes grown?
   A in a hedge   B in a bay   C in a field

9 Which of these is **not** on the coast?
   A harbour   B cliff   C countryside

10 Where would you be in the shade?
   A in a wood   B on the ocean   C in a desert

4 Complete sentences 1–5 with suitable weather words.

1 It's really .... – I can only see ten metres ahead of the car.

2 There was a heavy .... last night and the temperature was 8 degrees below ....

3 Will it stay .... all day or should I take an umbrella, in case it ....?

4 On the mountain top, we sat in warm .... , but we couldn't see anything below us because of a thin .... everywhere.

5 In a ...., you mustn't stand under a tree – it could be hit by ....!

5 Read 1–7 and complete the puzzle with a suitable adjective ending in *-ful* or *-able*. Then write a sentence including the eighth word that appears in the box.

1 The interview went well so I'm .... I'll get the job.

2 Glass, paper and metal can be used again – they are all ....

3 Franco likes seeing friends and meeting new people – he's very ....

4 Are the prices in the sports centre café .... , or are they very expensive?

5 You must be more .... when you're cooking – you've burnt the pan.

6 Don't leave anything .... in the changing room, as it isn't locked.

7 Mobile phones are really .... for finding out where your friends are.

```
1    _ _|_|_ _ _
2  _ _ _ _ _|_|_ _
3      _ _ _|_|_ _ _
4    _ _ _ _ _|_|_ _ _
5      _ _ _ _|_|_ _
6      _ _ _|_|_ _ _
7  _ _ _ _ _|_|
```

Writing

6 Match sentences 1–5 to functions a–e.

1 I decided not to go windsurfing because I didn't feel very well.
2 It was really nice of you to bake me a birthday cake.
3 Why don't we visit an art gallery together next weekend?
4 Please remember to register for the competition by next Friday.
5 I'm so sorry I couldn't join you at the restaurant.

a suggesting
b explaining
c apologising
d thanking
e reminding

7 Match tasks 1–3 to letter openings a–c and continue one of the letters. Close your letter with a suitable ending.

1 This is part of a letter you receive from a penfriend in Australia.

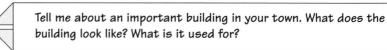

> Tell me about an important building in your town. What does the building look like? What is it used for?

Now write your penfriend a letter about an important building in your town.

2 This is part of a letter you receive from an English penfriend.

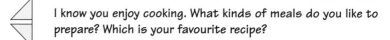

> I know you enjoy cooking. What kinds of meals do you like to prepare? Which is your favourite recipe?

Now write a letter, answering your penfriend's questions.

3 This is part of a letter you receive from your penfriend Marcello.

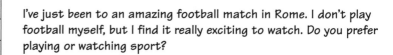

> I've just been to an amazing football match in Rome. I don't play football myself, but I find it really exciting to watch. Do you prefer playing or watching sport?

Now write a letter to Marcello about playing or watching sport.

a Dear Jane
You're right, I really love cooking. I make a lot of spicy dishes with rice and vegetables. Also, I make a lot of pasta, especially when I'm in a hurry. The meal I like doing most at the moment is...

b Dear Marcello
Lucky you! I feel the same as you, really. It's more fun to watch good players than to play a sport badly. The last sports event I went to was...

c Dear Brett
I suppose the most important building in town is the new concert hall. It's in a beautiful part of town and looks out over the river. The building's mainly steel and glass and it has four storeys altogether. On the ground floor, there's...

1

2

3

EXAM TASKS IN MODULE 3

Unit 10 – Paper 1 Reading Part 5
Unit 11 – Paper 3 Speaking Part 2
Unit 12 – Paper 2 Listening Part 4

Make sure you read the relevant parts of the Exam guide before doing these tasks.

Topics

1   What is happening in the photos? What topics do they show?

Vocabulary

2   Put the words into four groups. Then match three of the groups to topics in **1**.

adventure   angry   aunt   cooking   cousin
excited   father   horror   nephew   romance
running   sad   singing   thriller   walking
worried

Grammar

4

3   Match sentences 1–4 to a grammar area a–d and underline the word(s) that show you this.

1   I love spending time with my family.
2   You mustn't drive on the right in the UK.
3   Louisa had heard about Jem before they met on holiday last year.
4   'There are no towels in my room', Victor complained to the hotel manager.
    Victor complained that there were no towels in his room.

a   reported speech   c   verb + *-ing* form
b   past perfect   d   modal verbs

9.2 Leisure interests

Warm up

1 Discuss the questions.

- What are the most popular hobbies and interests in your country and the area you live in?
- What do the members of your family do in their free time?
- Do you think people's interests change during their life? If so, how?

Listening

2 Listen to seven short recordings. Match each one with a hobby or interest from the list. There are two extra items you do not need.

watching sports ☐
cooking ☐
wildlife ☐
keeping fit ☐
local information ☐
painting ☐
studying ☐
collecting things ☐
walking ☐

3 Listen and choose the correct picture for questions 1–6.

1 What exercise does Mary do?

A  B  C

2 What antique furniture does the woman have in her living room?

A  B  C

3 What food will the boy use?

A  B 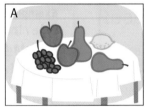 C

4 What can you see in the museum today?

A  B  C

5 Which picture does the woman like best?

A  B  C

6 Which evening class is the man going to take?

A  B  C

Vocabulary

→ VOCABULARY REFERENCE PAGE 123

4 Find the word in each list that is wrong and explain why it does not fit. What hobby or interest are the words connected with?

1 knife   kitchen   stamp   oven
2 screen   review   ticket   pencil
3 leaf   earth   plant   wing
4 audience   tent   band   guitarist
5 net   grill   racket   court
6 mountain   sewing   hat   snow
7 score   stadium   keyboard   supporter
8 curtain   draw   stage   stalls
9 paint   picture   match   brush
10 pool   needle   changing room   costume

5 Can you think of any more hobbies? Use the pictures to help.

6 Choose two of the hobbies from your list in **5** and write some notes about them to answer the questions.

- Where do these activities take place?
- What equipment do you need?
- What special skills or personal qualities do you need?

7 Tell a partner about the activities you chose.

Example

There are a lot of different places where you can climb – even indoors on a practice wall. You need ropes and other special equipment, including strong boots. If you go climbing, you need to be very fit and to be patient and calm. In this sport, you use your mind and your body together.

Speaking

8 Two friends have agreed to spend a day together at the weekend. Listen to their conversation and complete the spaces. What do they agree to do?

LENA Shall we go to the .... on Saturday afternoon?
GARY I'd prefer to do something outside. How about going to the .... ?
LENA I'm sorry. I really don't want to do that. We could go to the ....
GARY OK, that's a good idea. What about in the morning? Have you seen the .... exhibition in the museum?
LENA No, I haven't, but I've read about it. Yes, let's do that.

9 Underline the phrases Lena and Gary use to make and respond to suggestions.

10 You and your partner are going to spend a day together doing two of the activities shown below. Decide which two you want to do. Use the phrases from the dialogue to help you.

10.2 Screen scene

Warm up

1 What are your favourite three films? What type of films are they? Put them under the headings. Can you add any other films to the table?

adventure	comedy	drama	cartoon

horror	romance	science fiction	thriller

2 Describe the best bits of your favourite films.

Example
My favourite bit was when the main character jumped between two buildings.
The best bit was when Frodo and his friends fought against the Orcs.

Vocabulary

→ **VOCABULARY REFERENCE** PAGE 123

3 Read the examples and complete the rules with *-ed* or *-ing*.

The film was frightening. I was frightened.

The thing that frightens you is *frighten.........* .
The result is that you are *frighten.........* .

4 Make adjectives with the correct ending to complete sentences 1–8.

disappoint embarrass excite relax

1 I'm very .... about seeing the new *Lord of the Rings* film. The reviews were great.
2 Don't go and see the film on this week. It was terrible, really ....
3 We had very comfortable seats in the cinema and it was so warm that I felt very .... when we left.
4 The audience obviously didn't enjoy the film. The director was there – it was very .... for him.
5 All that excitement and action wasn't very .... , I was on the edge of my seat the whole time, but I did enjoy it.
6 The best bit was the car chase through Rome. It was really ....
7 I couldn't help crying in the cinema, but I was the only one and I was a bit .... about it.
8 We were .... that the main character acted so badly. She was fantastic in her last film.

Speaking

5 Study the two photos from films. Make notes about each scene.
- What type of film is it?
- Where does the scene take place?
- What are the people doing?
- What are their feelings?
- What is your reaction to the scene?

6 Work in pairs. Student A talks about the first scene using their notes from **5** and the phrases and ideas in the boxes below. Swap roles and Student B talks about the second scene. Can you add any other ideas?

Saying what you think about a picture and giving reasons

I think the scene must be from a … film, because …

I think he / she / they is/are feeling … because …

Describing location

The scene takes place
  outside, in a forest
  by the sea
  inside a café
  in a shopping centre

It looks like
  a lonely, dangerous place
  an expensive restaurant
  a house an old person lives in

Writing

7 Read Luca's letter to his English friend, John, about a film he has just seen. What type of film was it?

Dear John

Thank you for your letter. It was great to hear from you. Let me tell you about a film I saw last week called 'Flight of fright.' The story takes place in a small town in America. The people who live there start hearing voices and seeing strange things. Then they all see an insect as tall as a man, with huge wings.

The main character is a journalist who is visiting the town. He doesn't believe the stories, but after a few days, he has the same experiences.

It's a very exciting film with amazing special effects. We were really scared and everyone screamed when the insect man appeared.

Best wishes

Luca

8 In which paragraphs (1, 2 or 3) of Luca's letter can you find the answers to questions 1–6?

1 What is the name of the film?
2 When did Luca see it?
3 What did he think about the film?
4 Where does the story take place?
5 What is the story about?
6 Who is the main character?

9 Underline the adjectives in Luca's letter.

10 Complete sentences 1–8 with the adjectives.

dangerous   huge   lonely   new   old   scared
small   strange   surprised   tall

1 I don't know what bit me, but it was .... – really big, and very .... I'd never seen anything like it before.
2 The main character lived in a very .... flat and she and her four children all slept in the same bedroom.
3 Have you seen Steven Spielberg's .... film? It's only been out for two days and I've seen it twice!
4 Some actors aren't as .... as they look in films – they're really quite short.
5 After Clare had watched the horror film she was too .... to walk home on her own.
6 Some of things the actor had to do were so .... that another man acted in those scenes for him.
7 We were all .... at the end of the film – we didn't expect the hero to die.
8 The story is about a(n) .... woman in her 80s who has no friends or family and is very ....

11 You are going to write a letter to a friend about a film you've seen recently.

▼ Decide which film to write about.
▼ Make notes by thinking about the questions in **8**.
▼ Now decide on the best order for the information.
▼ Divide your notes into paragraphs.
▼ Choose a name for the person you're writing to.
▼ Follow your plan and notes and write your letter in about 100 words.

EXAM TIP Use adjectives to describe things correctly and to make your descriptions more interesting.

11.2 Take a break

Warm up

→ **VOCABULARY REFERENCE** PAGE 123

1 What sort of holiday is shown in each photo? How much luggage would you need for each one? Make lists of essential things to pack.

2 Discuss the questions.
- Which holiday would be the cheapest?
- Which would be the most challenging?
- Which would be the least enjoyable?

Listening

3 You will hear a radio presenter talking about holidays to the island of Madagascar. Before you listen, read sentences 1–6 and match each space to a–f.

a an activity b a day c a place d a month e a thing f a title

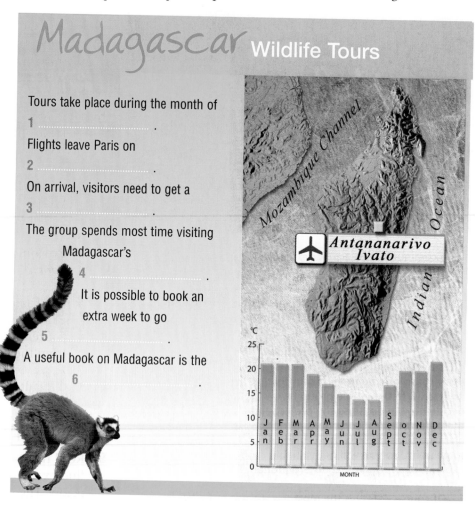

Madagascar Wildlife Tours

Tours take place during the month of

1 ....

Flights leave Paris on

2 ....

On arrival, visitors need to get a

3 ....

The group spends most time visiting Madagascar's

4 ....

It is possible to book an extra week to go

5 ....

A useful book on Madagascar is the

6 ....

> **EXAM TIP** You will hear the recording twice, so don't worry if you don't complete all the answers the first time you listen.

4 Listen to the recording and fill in the missing information.

5 Read the sentence below. This is a more natural way of saying 'a stay of two nights'. Do the same with 1–5.

Each tour starts with a *two-night stay*.
1 flight that takes twelve hours
2 a visa that lasts one month
3 a ferry crossing that is forty minutes long
4 a journey of 250 kilometres
5 an island that is 160 million years old

Speaking Part 2

→ EXAM GUIDE PAGE 118

6 You are going on a wildlife walking tour in Madagascar. Discuss why it would be useful to take each of the things below and suggest what else to pack. Agree on two extra things that are essential.

> **EXAM TIP** In Speaking Part 2 make sure you take turns with your partner. Keep the conversation going by asking each other about the reasons why you have suggested a particular solution to the task.

Writing

7 Match 1–5 to a–e and decide which of the five things in the picture in **6** they are describing.

1 Buy one that is up to date
2 These must be comfortable
3 You'll only need it
4 Covering your head is essential
5 You should use plenty

a to avoid sunstroke.
b to help you communicate.
c as bites can be painful.
d for the occasional shower.
e because you'll be walking every day.

8 Decide where the sentences in **7** fit in the text below.

> The first thing you must buy is a pair of proper walking shoes. .... In addition, you'll need a good sun hat. .... However, the weather conditions can be mixed, so it's a good idea to bring a rainproof jacket. .... Of course, a damp climate like this means insects, so pack several tubes of insect repellent. .... Last but not least, don't forget to include a French phrase book. ....

9 Match the underlined linking words and phrases in **8** to purposes 1–4.

1 adding contrasting or unexpected information
2 saying something is important despite its position in the paragraph
3 suggesting a second thing
4 highlighting a fact that is well-known

10 Which of these words are similar to 1–4 in **9**.

also   clearly   finally   on the other hand

11 Choose one of the holidays shown in **1**. Make a list of five essential things to take and decide why they are needed. Then write a paragraph like the one in **8**, using linking words. Write about 100 words.

12.2 Close to you

Speaking

→ **VOCABULARY REFERENCE** PAGE 124

1 Match questions 1–4 to answers a–d.

1 How do you get along with your family?
2 Which relationship means the most to you at the moment?
3 Are you closer to your family or your friends?
4 Which people do you share your secrets with?

a My family definitely, because they're the ones I'd turn to for help. I really enjoy hanging out with my friends, though I can't always depend on them!

b My brother's twelve years older, which means that we don't always get on with each other terribly well! On the other hand, I'm very close to my younger sister.

c I suppose there are two: Davy, my younger brother and Laura, my best friend at school – I tell her everything!

d That's an easy question to answer. My friend Kim – he has been great since Lizzy and I broke up, so he's very important in my life right now.

2 Discuss the questions.

- How important is the family in today's world?
- Can schoolfriends remain close in later life? Why / Why not?
- Should people form close relationships at work? Why / Why not?

Vocabulary

3 An extra preposition is sometimes added to 'two-part' phrasal verbs. Read the examples and find another three-part phrasal verb in **1** that works in this way.

James and his mates often *hang out* at the club.
James often *hangs out with* his mates at the club.

4 Match sentences 1–4 to the phrasal verb definitions a–d.

1 I met up with some old college friends on holiday.
2 Bettany walked out on her husband after she discovered him with another woman.
3 All Mike's friends have given up on him because he never keeps any promises.
4 Did you know that Lenny has split up with Jude?

a finish a relationship
b get together with someone
c stop trying to involve someone
d leave someone

5 Write sentences using two-part phrasal verbs from 1–4 in **4**.

8 Read the story and decide which first and second sentence in **6** it continues from. Don't worry about spaces 1–6 yet.

Now, as his eyes met hers, she 1 .... hoped that the girl had left. The band was playing 2 .... and they danced for ages. At the end, he took her back to her table and offered to buy her a drink, which she 3 .... accepted. While he was at the bar, a friend of hers came over. The friend warned her to watch out, as this guy Jonas 4 .... walked out on his girlfriends. She refused to listen because she 5 .... knew in her heart that they would be together forever. At the bar, Jonas was telling his sister, who he had brought to the club, 6 .... the same thing.

Writing

> **EXAM TIP** In Writing Part 3 if you are given the first sentence of a story, the rest of your story must be clearly connected to it.

6 Decide which second sentence a–e follows each first sentence 1–5. Think about the people in 1–5 and the pronouns in a–e.

1 Jane read Marc's letter again and smiled.
2 An extremely good-looking man asked Faye to dance.
3 On our first date, it was a very warm evening.
4 I don't regret leaving Jack.
5 The two lovers sat looking into each other's eyes.

a I had wanted to for years and that day, I finally did it.
b He was writing to tell her how much he loved her.
c Although they had only met the week before, it felt longer.
d She had seen him arrive at the club with a girl earlier.
e So we walked down to the river, where it was cooler.

7 Which second sentences in **6** use the past perfect tense? Why?

9 Put the adverbs into spaces 1–6 in **8** to improve the story.

already   exactly   happily   loudly   often   really

10 Match the third and fourth sentences a–h to the other four stories in **6** and put the adverbs in brackets into the correct place.

a Jane knew she could trust Marc. (completely)
b The water was clear and we could see our faces in it. (beautifully)
c Jack had been horrible to me the day after our wedding. (really)
d They thought the same way about so many things. (exactly)
e She decided to write back and tell him her own feelings. (immediately)
f He dropped a stone into the water and our faces disappeared for a moment. (suddenly)
g We were supposed to be flying to the Caribbean but he announced that the honeymoon would not take place. (nastily)
h They liked the same music, the same books, the same toothpaste! (even)

> **EXAM TIP** You can add interest to your writing by including adverbs. This will show your language range.

11 Your teacher has asked you to write a story. Choose one of the first sentences in **6** and finish the story in about 100 words.

Grammar

1 Complete the second sentence of each pair so that it means the same as the first, using no more than three words.

1 Lucy said it was the best play she had seen for ages.
Lucy said, 'It's the best play I .... for ages.

2 Dave and Linda prefer to stay in small hotels on holiday.
Dave and Linda .... staying in large hotels on holiday.

3 It's important to practise the piano if you want to play well.
You .... practise the piano if you want to play well.

4 'Let's go to the beach today instead of visiting another museum.'
Kate .... to the beach instead of visiting another museum.

5 Christine asked Rick if he'd enjoyed the film.
Christine asked Rick, ... the film?'

6 It's better to arrive at the airport before 11p.m.
Try to .... at the airport after 11p.m.

7 The first time I saw ancient buildings was in the Forum in Rome.
Until I visited the Forum in Rome, I .... any ancient buildings.

8 I didn't give Dave my phone number before I left the party.
I left the party without .... Dave my phone number.

9 Kay and I were friends before we fell in love.
Until we fell in love, Kay and I .... just been friends.

10 Tammy told Jed that she couldn't appear at the festival that year.
Tammy said, 'I .... at the festival this year.'

2 Choose the correct verb form for 1–12.

Two years ago Jim **1** *made / had* made a big decision which changed his life. He **2** *had / had had* a difficult time in the past few months. His marriage **3** *ended / had ended* after 10 years, and his wife **4** *moved / had moved* out of their house to live with her new partner. He was **5** *bored / had been bored* with his job, because he **6** *worked / had worked* for the same company for 15 years. The idea of moving abroad **7** *came / had come* suddenly. He **8** *always enjoyed / had always enjoyed* sailing, so he **9** *decided / had decided* to make it a way of life. He **10** *didn't / hadn't* owned a boat before, but he **11** *bought / had bought* the biggest one he could afford. Now he **12** *has been / had been* in Greece for almost two years, taking tourists on short cruises around the islands.

Writing

3 Complete this Entertainment guide with suitable adjectives from this list. Use each adjective once.

amazing   amusing   beautiful   best   friendly   funny
interested   interesting   talented   unexpected

WHAT'S ON

House party

An 1 .... film which will have you laughing from start to finish.

New World

A spaceship from Planet Earth discovers a new planet where 2 .... events happen that you just wouldn't predict. 3 .... special effects will keep you 4 .... the whole way through. Don't miss this film.

Viva Salsa

Join this 5 .... new dance club and meet lots of new people. Doors open at 8.30p.m. Watch 6 .... dancers and learn how to Salsa yourself.

Light and dark

An 7 .... exhibition of photographs taken at sunrise and sunset – 8 .... scenery.

An evening with Larry Stennick

This year's 9 .... comedian (he won two international prizes last month) will entertain you with 10 .... stories and jokes.

Vocabulary

4 Find eight adjectives and six prepositions in this word square. Match the adjectives to the prepositions to make phrases about feelings.

W	I	T	H	U	I	W	K	I	N	B	M
G	Q	O	L	N	Y	A	J	P	L	X	A
D	I	S	A	P	P	O	I	N	T	E	D
V	C	U	F	L	R	T	B	J	W	M	K
A	H	T	D	E	W	B	I	E	O	P	G
V	T	C	R	A	Z	Y	C	A	H	T	F
J	E	L	D	S	W	A	U	L	X	P	O
D	F	Y	E	A	M	B	B	O	O	W	N
H	O	V	P	N	W	O	G	U	T	S	D
R	D	L	T	T	I	U	M	S	E	C	E
N	Y	O	F	D	G	T	B	O	R	E	D

5 Complete the text by adding one of these words.

hour   minute   night   star   year

Enjoy a ¹ three-............... break in Cordoba in southern Spain. Stay in a luxury ² five- .... hotel in the heart of this beautiful ³ 1200- .... old city. Take a walking tour round the sights, or join a trip to the ruins of a Moorish palace only a ⁴ 20- .... taxi ride from the city. Taste the local food in the many excellent resaurants and watch the traditional flamenco dancing in a ⁵ one- .... show.

6 Add words to this spidergram on hobbies and interests.

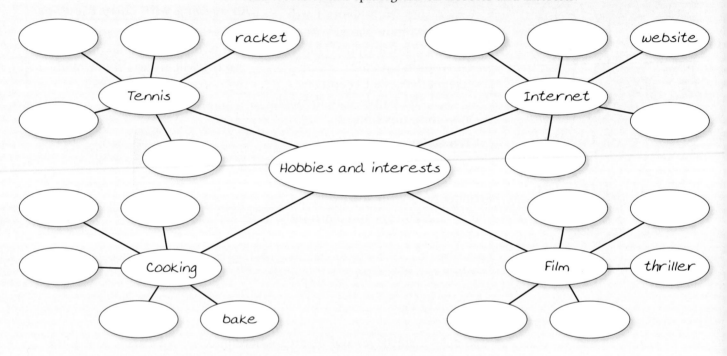

7 Answer questions 1–3 using these words.

a break   direction   money   place   roles   time   turns

1 What can you spend?
2 What can change?
3 What can you take?

8 Use the verb-noun phrases from **7** to complete 1–7.

1 How much .... did you .... into Australian dollars before you went to Sydney?
2 The taxi driver suddenly .... and Tom was thrown against the door.
3 Shall we .... from our work and get something to eat?
4 I can't believe how much .... I .... on going out last month – I'll have to stay in and watch TV
5 What month does the annual film festival .... ?
6 Valerie doesn't want to be the team leader any more – would you .... with her and let her do the cooking tomorrow?
7 There were two guides on the tour who .... to give the evening lecture and guide us during the day.

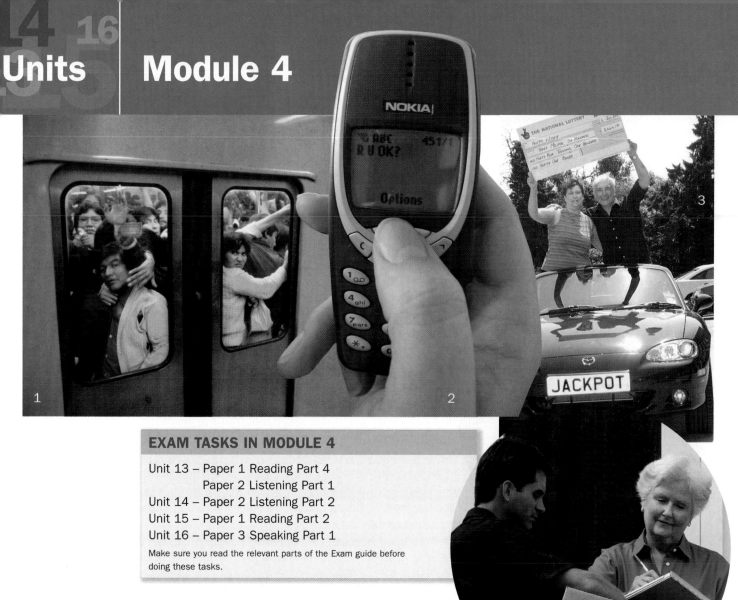

Topics

1 What is happening in the photos?
What topics do they show?

Vocabulary

2 Match these words to the photos in **1.**
box   excited   miserable   pleased   prize   technology   thumb   train

Grammar

3 Match sentences 1–4 to a grammar area a–d and underline the word(s) that show you this.

1 I'll pass on your message when he gets back.

3 We're going to have a holiday in Corsica next year.

2 If I won the lottery, I'd stop working.

4 I used to travel to college by bus.

a using a conditional structure
b talking about a definite future plan
c talking about the past
d making a promise about the future

13.1 Your own wheels

Reading Part 4

➜ **EXAM GUIDE** PAGE 111

3 Read the text and questions below.
For each question, mark the letter next to the correct answer – A, B, C or D.

The travel choices of **young adults**

The topic of travel at the stage when teenagers become old enough to drive, go to university or start a job has received little public or government attention. Yet it is essential to encourage young adults to make sensible choices, given that traffic is becoming worse and worse.

In Britain, a lot of young people start using family cars or running their own car as soon as they can. It's easy to see why. In their early teens, many have depended on the car and know the disadvantages of bus and rail travel from personal experience. By contrast, teenagers are given a positive view of driving through TV advertising, and know nothing about the problems of car use.

Traditional attitudes to transport do often change once young adults move to new places and meet new people, such as at university. Research suggests, for example, that cycling is seen as a childish activity, although a general cycling culture in Oxford and Cambridge encourages students there to use bikes. Some British universities have banned students from bringing cars on site and instead provide buses to important destinations. One university even has special night buses with security guards on board, picking students up from nightclubs as late as 3a.m.

Not everyone wants to join their friends and own a car, even though parents often offer to pay for driving lessons. Many cannot afford to buy one, while a growing number are against cars altogether, saying what they produce is bad for the environment. Whatever their opinion, one thing is certain: travel habits are hard to break, so young adults need to be shown which transport choices will be sustainable over the next twenty years.

Warm up

1 Which of the forms of transport in the photos do you prefer? Why?

2 How important is it to have your own transport? What are the benefits? What are the problems?

1 Why has the writer written this text?
   A to complain about the attitudes of today's youth
   B to discuss an issue that is important for young people
   C to explain why so many students travel around
   D to describe the various benefits of owning a car

2 The writer thinks that many British children
   A enjoy travelling to school by bus or by train.
   B learn about the negative side of cars from their parents.
   C grow up feeling that a car is essential in their lives.
   D are annoyed by car advertisements on television.

3 What does the writer say about transport choices at British universities?

A Travelling by bus at night is unsafe at one particular university.

B Cycling isn't considered a suitable form of transport at any university.

C There aren't enough buses at universities where cars are prohibited.

D When they reach university, many students reconsider how they travel.

4 According to the writer, more young people are refusing to drive because

A they believe that pollution caused by cars is dangerous.

B they don't have enough money to keep a car on the road.

C their parents persuade them it is unnecessary to learn.

D their friends are able to give them lifts everywhere.

5 What advice would the writer give to someone of 18?

A You've managed to get through life without a family car, like most families. Carry on using your bike, it's safer!

B Why don't you learn to drive before you start at university? It's possible to take a car on site at all universities.

C Although a car might be convenient to you now, you must think about the future before you choose whether to get one or not.

D Don't worry about saving for a car, you can continue to depend on the bus like you always have!

Grammar

Will / shall

➔ **GRAMMAR REFERENCE** PAGE 132

4 Read examples 1–3. Which one contains an offer and which one a promise? Is the remaining example a prediction or a plan?

1 If you want to learn to drive, I'll pay for your lessons.

2 Traffic in cities will get worse and worse unless something is done now.

3 We'll give you a ring as soon as we get home.

5 Predict what will happen in the future on each of issues 1–5, using *will* or *won't*.

Example

petrol prices *Petrol prices will go up.*

1 traffic in city centres
2 car advertisements
3 pollution levels
4 public transport
5 car design

6 Make offers or promises in answer to 1–6, using the short form *I'll*.

Example

The car needs petrol. *I'll get some at the garage.*

1 Donna wants a lift to the party.
2 We can't hear the radio in the back.
3 Your sister wants to see you.
4 Helen thinks she's left her car keys here.
5 You'll need to be here by ten o'clock.
6 Will there be a car space for me next week?

Writing

7 Read the task, exam tip and the pairs of sentences. Which sentence is better for each point? Why?

Your American friend Dale is coming to stay with you next Saturday and you plan to meet him at the airport.

Write an email to Dale. In your email, you should

- ask him what time he will arrive on Saturday
- offer to meet him at the airport
- explain your plans for Saturday evening.

> **EXAM TIP** Where possible, you should avoid using the words given in the task instructions, to show your own range of language.

1 A What time will you arrive on Saturday?
   B When will your flight get in on Saturday?

2 A I'll meet you at the airport.
   B I'll pick you up from the airport, of course.

3 A If you're not too tired, we'll go out to a nice restaurant on Saturday evening.
   B My plans on Saturday evening are to have a meal together.

8 Write an answer to this task, in 35–45 words.

Your friend Kim needs a lift to a party tonight.

Write an email to Kim. In your email, you should

- offer to give Kim a lift to the party
- make an arrangement to meet her
- remind her what your car looks like.

14.1 Free to talk

Warm up

1 What are the advantages and disadvantages of mobile phones? Put these points into two groups, positive (+) and negative (−), and add ideas of your own.

- convenient to carry around
- expensive to use
- attractive to thieves
- cheap texting facility
- easy to lose
- good in an emergency
- noisy in public places

Vocabulary

2 Using a dictionary if necessary, decide which verb is the odd one out in groups 1–8 and say why.

1 say/talk/shout/tell
2 discover/display/invent/research
3 ban/delay/forbid/prevent
4 forward/receive/send/fax
5 dream/imagine/insist/think
6 do/make/prepare/win
7 accept/allow/approve/refuse
8 change/wait/remain/stay

3 Choose the correct noun in sentences 1–6.

1 The whole mobile phone *industry / company* is experiencing problems, with sales down worldwide.
2 Someone left you a *message / speech* about half an hour ago.
3 The *custom / habit* of giving chocolate eggs at Easter is popular throughout Europe.
4 If you can't hear what I'm saying, try to read my *lips / mouth*.
5 Scientists are picking up a faint radio *sign / signal* from space.
6 The *price / prize* of that new phone is very high.

Reading

4 Read the text about a new type of mobile phone that is being developed. What is different about it? Don't worry about spaces 1–10 yet.

PRIVATE **CONVERSATIONS**

Wherever they are, some people insist on shouting into their mobile phones. It's hard to 1 .... these users breaking their bad habit, but one Japanese 2 .... is going to try to persuade them. Researchers at this firm are 3 .... the world's first lip-reading mobile phone. Although 4 .... a long way off, this phone should prevent anyone 5 .... having to shout, even in a noisy place. All the users will have to 6 .... is to say the words silently and the phone will change the message made by 7 .... moving lips into speech or text. The phone works by 8 .... tiny electrical signals from around the user's mouth. The engineers are proud of 9 .... they have designed and believe that the phone will be a commercial success within five years. As mobiles are 10 .... on some public transport networks in Japan, this is welcome news.

> **EXAM TIP** In Reading Part 5 look at the words before and after the spaces to help you choose the correct word.

5 Complete the text by choosing the correct word for each space.

	A		B		C		D	
1	A	think	B	imagine	C	dream	D	hope
2	A	industry	B	factory	C	club	D	company
3	A	displaying	B	developing	C	drawing	D	describing
4	A	still	B	already	C	ever	D	yet
5	A	for	B	by	C	from	D	with
6	A	make	B	get	C	do	D	keep
7	A	its	B	his	C	our	D	their
8	A	receiving	B	fetching	C	putting	D	bringing
9	A	which	B	what	C	who	D	where
10	A	refused	B	stopped	C	banned	D	cancelled

Speaking

→ VOCABULARY REFERENCE PAGE 124

6 What methods of communication are shown in pictures 1–6? Which do you prefer and why? Give two reasons, choosing from the ones below or adding your own. Use a linking phrase before you give the second reason.

Giving reasons for preferences

I prefer … because … I can use it anywhere.
       … it doesn't cost much.
       … it's more personal.
       … it takes less time.
       … I like to see who I'm talking to.
       … I can send attachments.
       … I can contact several people quickly.

And besides, …
Apart from that, …
Also, …
Secondly, …
More importantly, …

7 Decide which method of communication is best for situations 1–5, choosing each method once only. Explain the reasons for your choice.

1 changing arrangements at the last minute
2 informing someone of some bad news
3 apologising for a mistake you have made
4 letting everyone know your new address
5 finding out whether your friend is feeling better

Writing

8 Read the task, the exam tip and the sample answer. Does it answer both of the penfriend's questions? What's missing? What shouldn't be there?

> **EXAM TIP** In Writing Part 3 you only need to write about 100 words so only include information you are asked for.

• This is part of a letter you receive from an English penfriend.

> I've just bought a mobile phone and I'm finding it very useful! How useful do you think mobile phones are? What don't you like about them?

• Now write a letter, answering your penfriend's questions.

> Dear André
> Thanks for your letter. I don't have a mobile phone at the moment. It was stolen recently. I think a mobile is very useful. You can use it anywhere. If there's an emergency you can phone for an ambulance. You can text your friends. I'll have to buy another one soon. How are you? I'm fine. I went to a great party last Saturday and all my friends were there. We danced all night. It was fantastic.
> Pete

9 The sample answer is 77 words long. Rewrite it, cutting what shouldn't be there and including anything that is missing. The final letter should be about 100 words.

14.2 Disappearing languages

France · Italy · Provence · Mediterranean sea · Corsica

Warm up

1 Do you recognise any of these languages or dialects?

1 pishkado kon guevo i limon
2 Qu'es aco?
3 a roba face u prezzu
4 è comu u vermu 'ndo fummagiu
5 Fins demà!

2 How many languages are spoken in your country? Are dialects in your country more or less important than they used to be? Why?

Vocabulary

3 Match each pair of words to their definitions (A or B).

flag / signpost
dictionary / grammar
dialect / language
local / traditional

1 connected to communication
A the form of speech used in a particular area
B the standard way of communicating in a country or region

2 reference books
A this publication explains the rules of a language
B this book gives the meaning or translations of words

3 belonging to an area
A used to describe an ancient and unchanged custom or belief
B used to describe the places near your home

4 types of signal
A a coloured piece of cloth which is often flown outside
B something that displays information about destinations

Listening Part 2

→ **EXAM GUIDE** PAGE 115

4 You will hear a woman talking about Provençal, a language that used to be commonly spoken in the south of France.
For each question, put a tick (✔) in the correct box.

1 The Provençal village of Cabasse is unusual because
   A of its ancient streets and buildings. ☐
   B its name is displayed in two languages. ☐
   C people still collect water from its fountain. ☐

2 Most people living in Provence today come from
   A within the area itself. ☐
   B other parts of Europe. ☐
   C North Africa. ☐

3 The Provençal flag is partly
   A blue. ☐
   B yellow. ☐
   C white. ☐

4 The language of Provençal is mainly spoken
   A among friends. ☐
   B by shopkeepers. ☐
   C within the family. ☐

5 What, according to Annie, shows that Provençal is still popular?
   A a range of dictionaries ☐
   B a daily radio programme ☐
   C a newly-published translation ☐

6 What used to happen when children spoke Provençal at school?
   A They were told to leave the school immediately. ☐
   B They had to play outside instead of attending classes. ☐
   C They received an embarrassing punishment. ☐

5 Should people try to keep regional languages alive? What role should the government have in this?

Grammar

Used to

→ **GRAMMAR REFERENCE** PAGE 133

6 Read the example. Is the fountain the only location for water now?

The village fountain *used to* be the only location for water.

We use *used to* to talk about things which happened in the past but don't now.

7 Describe the changes shown in pictures 1–4, using *used to*.

Example
Our cat used to be small, but now he's enormous!

1

2

3

4

8 Read the information in the table. Then ask and answer 1–8.

negative	questions with *did*	'wh' questions without *did*
Children didn't *use to* speak Provençal at school.	Did more people *use to* speak Corsican? How did you *use to* get to school?	What language *used to* be the most common here?

Example
your grandparents/speak in dialect   Did
Did your grandparents use to speak in dialect?
They used to speak in dialect to each other, but they didn't use to speak it in public.

1   you / work hard at primary school   Did
2   you / watch cartoons on television   Did
3   Bill Clinton / president of the USA   Did
4   Roberto Baggio / play in the Italian team   Did
5   your favourite band / three years ago   What
6   Madonna / dress   How
7   food / like when you were younger   What
8   you / eat with your whole family   When

9 Make tag questions for 1–4 in **8**.

Example
Your grandparents used to speak in dialect, didn't they?

Warm up

→ **VOCABULARY REFERENCE** PAGE 124

1 Which of these things do you or your family do for yourselves? Which do other people do for you?

- clean the windows
- mend your computer
- wash your clothes
- prepare meals
- cut your hair
- do the housework
- repair the car
- check your teeth are healthy
- walk your dog

2 What other services do you and your family use? Why do you use them?

Grammar

Have / get something done

→ **GRAMMAR REFERENCE** PAGE 133

3 Complete the table.

subject	*have* or *get*	object	past participle	extra information
I	have/get	my hair	....	at Paolo's salon.
James	....	his teeth	....	twice a year.
We	....	our house	....	every week.

4 Say what Laura had done last week. Don't forget to use the past participle of the main verb.

Example
On Monday she had her living room painted.

MONDAY	THURSDAY
painter – living room	eye test

TUESDAY	FRIDAY
hair cut	a.m. cleaner

WEDNESDAY	SATURDAY
p.m. car repair	photo for passport

Vocabulary

5 Make phrases from the verbs and nouns. Then use them in the correct tense to complete sentences 1–8. Some nouns can be used with more than one verb.

book	an appointment the bill a complaint a flight
make	a holiday a meal something through the post
order	a reservation a room a table tickets
pay	

1 That restaurant is always busy on Friday evenings. You'd better
....

2 The train was an hour and a half late; I'm going to
....

3 Nina phoned her boyfriend in Australia every day. She had to get a job in order to ....

4 Have you .... for next month's concert yet?

5 My mother .... a dress .... and when it came it was two sizes too big.

6 Hello. I'd like to .... from your Winter Ski brochure, please.

7 Could I .... to see the doctor on Friday?

8 I'd like to .... in your hotel for the nights of 21st and 22nd July.

Listening

6 Underline the letters we do not pronounce in these words.

climb cupboard doubt foreign guide hour island knock night talk thought Wednesday wrong

7 Can you think of five other words with silent letters?

8 You will hear a recorded message about a hostel. Listen and fill in the missing information. When you have finished, check that you have spelt the words correctly.

> **EXAM TIP** In Listening Part 3 you must spell the answers correctly.

QUAYSIDE INTERNATIONAL HOSTEL
Close to town centre, beach and
(1) .... Kitchen, dining room, TV lounge,
small garden
(2) .... and wardrobes in the rooms
Put your valuable belongings in a locker
Basement – (3) .... , space for
drying clothes
Barbecues, parties, trips
Food – (4) .... tea, coffee and
biscuits
Pick up from (5) .... or train station
Cost – £18 per (6) .... , £80 for a
week, £25 per person in a double room

Speaking

9 Read the description of the picture. Match parts of the text to these words and phrases, then make new sentences.

a beard will be bald he's a barber customer a hairbrush and combs razor shaved

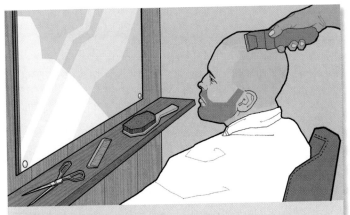

The man is having his hair cut. He won't have any hair left on his head. The other man is using a special piece of equipment to do this. It's his job to cut hair. That's why the first man doesn't look worried about it. The first man has got hair on his chin. Perhaps he will have this cut as well. In front of them there are things for making your hair look tidy. The man won't need them any more.

10 Describe what you can see in the photos. Use the description in **9** for ideas about how to talk about something when you do not know the exact words.

> **EXAM TIP** If you don't know a particular word, find other words to say what's happening.

15.2 Student life

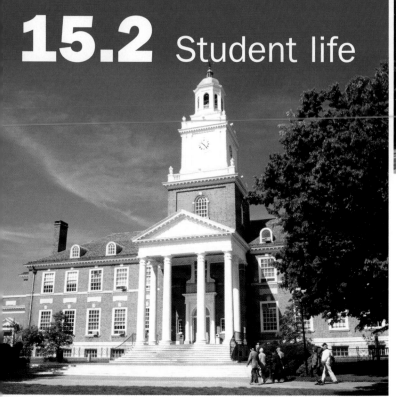

Warm up

1 Have you ever thought about going abroad to study? Discuss the questions.

- Which country would you prefer to study in?
- What will you study?
- Where will you live?
- Would you cook for yourself or eat in the university's restaurant?

Grammar

Future forms

→ **GRAMMAR REFERENCE** PAGE 133

2 Underline the verbs used to give a future meaning in sentences 1–5 and match them to uses a–e.

1 Anneka gets good marks for every essay – she's going to get an excellent degree.
2 Lee: The printer's not working.
  Kim: I'll have a look at it.
3 Lee's lent me a dictionary. I'm going to translate that lovely poem for Kirsten.
4 Professor Nilson will be at the conference to talk about his work on animal behaviour.
5 I'm working as a tour guide in the summer holidays.

a intention decided before speaking
b a decision made at the time of speaking
c definite arrangement in the future
d prediction based on evidence
e certainty about future situations

3 Read sentences 1–10 and correct any mistakes.

1 I've got some college brochures. I'll do a language course abroad this year.
2 Tim is being here soon.
3 Fran will leave college if she can't change her course.
4 Harry'll buy a new car soon. His old one is getting very unreliable.
5 It's going to be great to see you again.
6 That ladder doesn't look very safe. Someone will have a nasty accident.
7 I saw Shona yesterday. She'll have a baby.
8 Joe's going to study in Australia. He's got a place on a course in Melbourne.
9 The doorbell's ringing. I'm going to go and see who it is.
10 Is that coat really only £35? I'm going to buy it.

Writing

4 Read Kristin's note to Viv. Why is it rather boring?

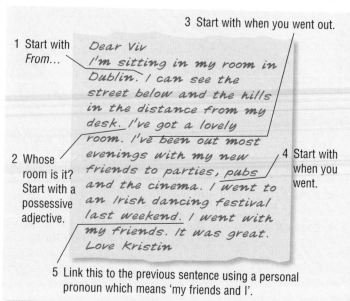

1 Start with From...

Dear Viv
I'm sitting in my room in Dublin. I can see the street below and the hills in the distance from my desk. I've got a lovely room. I've been out most evenings with my new friends to parties, pubs and the cinema. I went to an Irish dancing festival last weekend. I went with my friends. It was great.
Love Kristin

2 Whose room is it? Start with a possessive adjective.

3 Start with when you went out.

4 Start with when you went.

5 Link this to the previous sentence using a personal pronoun which means 'my friends and I'.

5 Rewrite the letter starting each sentence differently, using the prompts.

Example

1 *From my desk I can see the street below and the hills in the distance.*

6 The people below all want to study abroad.
Decide which university (A–H) would be the most suitable for each person (1–5).

1 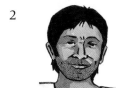 Fatima would like to spend a few days learning about university life at the start of her studies. She would like to be able to go home regularly to see her family.

2  Luis is worried about having to look for a room for himself. He's keen to study other subjects apart from his main course.

3 Jeanne is quite shy but wants to make new friends. She would prefer contact with individuals, but is happy to join in groups doing a planned activity.

4  Carlos is interested in finding out about the history of places and experiencing customs, such as typical dishes. He doesn't mind where he lives.

5  Stefan likes to explore the countryside when he's not studying. He is happier learning in a class with only a few other students.

STUDY ABROAD

A **Trinity College Dublin**
Dublin is a capital city with much to explore and a young population to meet. Stay in a university room in your first week while you are looking for accommodation. Eat in town or enjoy a traditional dinner served every evening at 6.15p.m.

B **Manchester**
The University offers a five-day Introduction Course for international students to help you feel at home with us. Manchester is a successful commercial city with a very active social and cultural life. It's close to an international airport with good connections worldwide.

C **Edinburgh**
Welcome to Scotland's beautiful capital. Learn about the city's history and university at our International Day. Meet British students at the Tandem Society where you'll be given a 'Tandem partner' who is there to help you. Tandem also organises events such as trips and nights out.

D **Warwick**
We send out a Welcome Guide to all international students. It will help you to prepare for your study in the UK and you can read about life at the university. When you apply for accommodation, please tell us if you want to do your own cooking or eat in one of the restaurants in the university.

E **York**
Enjoy living only a short journey from an ancient city. We can offer accommodation for the whole of your course. While you're here, why not take extra courses, for example, communication skills or business knowledge.

F **Brighton**
Study by the seaside! Students will meet you for our free airport pick-up service from the London airports. A team of staff is ready to help you with any questions or problems. Extra English language lessons are offered if you need them.

G **Aberdeen**
A busy city with close connections to the oil and gas industry, but it only takes 30 minutes to reach beaches, forests and hills. We have excellent staff-student relationships and have small classes. There are more than 1,000 computers for students to use.

H **Bath**
Bath is a city rich in cultural festivals – literature, music and film. Join us for the Welcome Evening, where teachers will talk to small groups to give you information about British customs, living in the UK, and ask about your English language needs. We run a bus service from the airport at the start of the course.

16.1 It could happen to you ...

Warm up

1 Match the expressions to photos 1–5. More than one expression can be used with some pictures.

I'm so happy for you!   What's the matter?
I'm so sorry.   I hope you get better soon.
What happened?   Congratulations!   Well done!
That's great news.   Never mind.

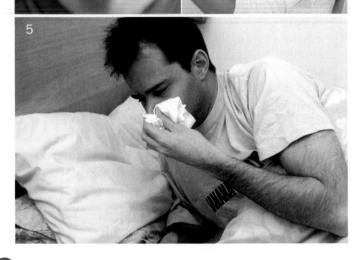

Reading

2 Read messages 1–4. What are they about?

Example
1 new job

1
> I've got the job at the lawyer's office! The interview went much better than at the library and they offered me the job today.
>
> Fran

2
> Jan phoned. She can't see you tonight. Her sister has just had a baby and she wants to see them both. She'll phone back later.

3
> *Paul and Lucy are moving to 12 High Street, Bridgetown, on Friday 10th February. No phone there yet, so please call our mobiles.*

4
> Pattie
> Grandma came out of hospital today and is back at home. She'd love to see you. She said you can visit any time.
> Rachel

3 Correct sentences 1–12 to give true information about the messages in **2**.

1 The new job is at the library.
2 The interview at the library went well.
3 The new job started today.
4 Jan was planning to go out with her sister this evening.
5 Jan is going to phone her sister about the baby.
6 Jan's sister is going to phone later.
7 Paul and Lucy have moved to a new house.
8 They moved on 10th February.
9 They will not have a phone at their new house.
10 Grandma's back in hospital.
11 Please visit her today.
12 Grandma wants Rachel to visit her.

Speaking Part 1

→ **EXAM GUIDE** PAGE 117

4 Work in pairs. Student A turn to page 107. Student B turn to page 108. Follow the instructions on your page.

Grammar

Second conditional

→ **GRAMMAR REFERENCE** PAGE 134

5 Read the text and complete sentences 1–3 with words from it.

LIFE choices

LIFE CHOICES presents readers with real-life situations and asks what decisions you would make. Last week we asked you if you would ever lie. We all like to think we're honest, but are there situations in which even the most trustworthy of us would bend the truth? This is what you told us.

Fran: If I really wanted a job and didn't have exactly the right qualifications, then I would lie and say I had got them. If I was confident about my ability to do the job, it wouldn't matter if I wasn't completely truthful.

Kerry: I think I might lie if a friend asked me to. If he had done something he shouldn't, and I knew about it, then I wouldn't tell anyone. Your friends are important, and I'd expect him to do the same for me.

Mark: I don't like the idea of lying at all. But if the only way I could protect my family was to tell a lie, then I would. My family comes before everything, even the truth.

1 Fran would lie if she .... the right qualifications for a job.
2 If a friend .... Kerry to keep a secret, she wouldn't tell anyone.
3 If Mark needed to protect his family, he .... tell a lie.

6 Answer questions 1–6 about the people in the text.

1 Has Fran got a new job?
2 Has Fran told a lie?
3 What has Kerry's friend done?
4 Is Kerry keeping a secret for her friend?
5 Is Mark's family in trouble?
6 Has Mark lied to help his family?

7 Underline two modal verbs in what Kerry and Mark say which can replace *would* and complete the rule about the second conditional.

We use the second conditional to talk about situations which don't exist or are unlikely to exist. In the *if* clause we use the .... tense, and in the main clause we use .... + infinitive. We can also use .... and .... in the main clause.

8 Discuss the questions.
* Would you ever start an argument with someone?
* Would you ever walk out on a relationship?
* Would you ever cheat in an exam?
* Would you ever lie to your best friend?

→ **VOCABULARY REFERENCE** PAGE 124

9 Discuss how you would feel and what you would do in situations 1–6 below. Use these adjectives and verbs and any of your own.

Adjectives
afraid   angry   anxious   delighted   depressed
disappointed   embarrassed   excited   miserable
nervous   sad   satisfied   worried

Verbs
apologise   argue   blame   choose   discuss   feel
lie   persuade

Example
If someone knocked on my door in the middle of the night, I would …
If someone knocked on my door in the middle of the night, I would feel nervous and worried. I would look out of the window to see who it was.

1 If I failed my driving test, I would …
2 If I waited half an hour in the rain for a friend who didn't come, I'd …
3 If my ex-boy / girlfriend got engaged, I would …
4 If I drove into my neighbour's car, I would …
5 If I was offered two jobs on the same day, I'd …

16.2 Life can be difficult

20-something and in the red

THE NUMBER of young people in debt in the UK is growing. Student loans, the high cost of accommodation, spending on credit cards and buying lottery tickets are all contributing to the increasing levels of debt these unhappy 20-somethings are experiencing. Some are just careless with money, most have no idea how to manage it properly. Organisations which offer advice on how to deal with debt are busier than ever. Advisors help their clients to draw up a 'debt management plan' to work out how to make repayments and keep spending to a minimum. Those in real difficulties find themselves with plans which last for 10–15 years – not a great start to adult life.

Warm up

1 Read the short text and answer the questions.
   1 What problem is the text about?
   2 What can cause this problem?
   3 What solution is described?

2 Find words in the text which mean the same as 1–3.
   1 money that you owe to somebody
   2 money that somebody lends to you
   3 buying goods or services you pay for later

3 Make notes on ways you think young people could reduce how much money they spend. Then in pairs, give each other some advice on cutting your spending. Use *should*.

Example
You should eat at home more often.

Vocabulary

→ **VOCABULARY REFERENCE** PAGE 124

4 Find a word beginning with *un-* and one ending in *-less* in the text in **1**. Which affix is used to mean *without* and which is used to make the opposite of a word?

5 Complete sentences 1–8 with the words, adding *un-* or *-less* where necessary.

   ashamed   attractive   care   fear   happy   heart   pleasant   worried

   1 Bobby won't apologise to Mary for telling the manager who wrote her report. He seems .... of what he's done.
   2 We had a really .... time at Kate's last night. She cooked a delicious meal and we chatted and laughed a lot.
   3 Jackie has been really .... about her break-up with Nick – she hasn't thought about his feelings at all.
   4 When Ray saw how .... I was about failing my exam, he took me out to cheer me up.
   5 Silvi is so .... She's always forgetting her keys and locking herself out.
   6 Did you see that programme on rock-climbing? They didn't use any special equipment and climbed up rocks hundreds of metres high – they're completely ....
   7 I'd hate to work in that bank. They have really .... uniforms.
   8 I'm a bit .... about Robert. I haven't seen him for ages and he hasn't returned any of my phone calls.

Listening

6 You will hear two friends talking about someone they know. Listen and say why Sally is worried about Henry.

7 Listen again and rewrite sentences 1–5 so that the information is correct.

1 John thinks Henry is generally fit.
2 Sally wants Henry to go to her house on Saturday evening.
3 Henry normally spends a lot of time at home at the weekend.
4 Henry has told Sally all about his training.
5 John suggests persuading Henry to stop training.

8 What do you think Sally and John should do about Henry?

Writing

9 Read the story and choose the most suitable title for it from the list. Why are the other titles unsuitable?

A new friend   A bad day
An enjoyable journey   Lost and found
A difficult conversation

Christina met a friendly young woman at the bus stop one day. They sat together on the bus and talked for the whole journey. Christina was happy when she got to work because she had really enjoyed their conversation.
At lunchtime she wanted to buy a sandwich, but couldn't find her purse. Suddenly she remembered the stranger. The woman had admired her bag and had picked it up to look at it. Christina was sure she had stolen her purse. She was very angry. The money didn't matter, but the purse did. A very good friend had given it to her for her birthday and now it was lost forever.

10 What tense is used to tell most of the story? What other tenses are used and why?

11 Find 14 incorrect tenses in the story below and correct them.

The *birthday* present

ON SATURDAY I was going shopping for something to wear to a party that night. It was Belinda's birthday, so I had needed to get a present to take to the party, too. It rained, so I have taken the bus into town. I was buying Belinda a really nice scarf and got some wrapping paper and a funny card. When I had got home I had been tired, but I was very happy because I found just the right trousers and shirt. I had a shower, was ironing my new clothes and had got ready for the party. I looked for the scarf to wrap up for Belinda when I was realising that I left it in the shop. Our local shop was the only one still open, so I had bought some chocolates on my way to the party.

12 Write a story with the title 'A day to remember'. Think about

- where you were, or where you went
- what happened
- what you felt about it and why you remember it.

Write about 100 words.

EXAM TIP When you write a story be very careful to use the correct tenses.

Grammar

1 Complete the second sentence of each pair so that it means the same as the first, using no more than three words.

1 Kieran said he would email his report next Thursday.
Kieran said 'I .... report next Thursday'.
2 In the past, the village had a spring festival, but not any more.
The village .... have a spring festival.
3 The garage is going to check the brakes for me.
I'm going to .... checked by the garage.
4 Traffic jams are unavoidable at this time of day.
You can't .... traffic jams at this time of day.
5 Sandra won't speak to you again unless you apologise.
If you apologised, Sandra .... to you again.
6 Marcia asked her uncle if he had gone fishing as a boy.
Marcia asked her uncle 'Did you .... go fishing as a boy?'
7 I'm going to walk to the stadium tomorrow evening.
I'm going to get to the stadium .... tomorrow evening.
8 Every three years, someone repaints the doors and windows for us.
Every three years, we .... the doors and windows repainted.
9 Harry is so in debt that he'll have to cancel his holiday.
Harry has .... large debt that he'll have to cancel his holiday.
10 The helicopter is quicker than the ferry.
It takes .... by helicopter than by ferry.

2 Find 14 words to do with language and communication in this wordsearch. The words run from left to right and top to bottom. Use some of the words in sentences 1–5 below.

D	O	S	P	E	E	C	H	D	S	H	A
I	T	E	X	T	U	S	P	O	K	E	N
A	S	H	O	U	T	E	S	D	D	U	B
L	A	T	H	S	P	U	B	L	I	S	H
E	O	A	L	I	E	R	Y	S	C	Q	U
C	S	G	E	G	C	H	A	T	T	U	A
T	T	R	A	N	S	L	A	T	I	O	N
S	I	A	O	A	P	L	T	G	O	T	A
L	V	M	L	L	O	T	L	W	N	A	T
E	A	M	I	S	M	E	S	S	A	G	E
A	L	A	P	T	P	L	E	T	R	W	L
F	I	R	S	G	I	L	A	L	Y	U	T

1 Have you .... much Swedish since you left Stockholm?
2 The company is going to .... a new English .... of Pirandello's plays.
3 Why not send a .... to Carlos? He'll definitely have his mobile on.
4 If looked up more words in a .... , your spelling would improve.
5 Are you free for a quick .... ? I want to .... you all about my trip.

Vocabulary

3 Choose the correct option for 1–8.

1 Which of these travels on the sea?

   A tram   B train   C hydrofoil

2 How would you feel if your car was stolen?

   A happy   B angry   C embarrassed

3 Where would you go to have some flowers sent to a relative?

   A a florist's   B a café   C the drycleaner's

4 What can you order in advance?

   A laundry   B faxes   C pizza

5 Which of these is **not** connected with a hairdresser's?

   A locker   B barber   C customer

6 What would you do if somebody threw water all over you?

   A apologise to him   B agree with him   C shout at him

7 How did people used to travel 200 years ago?

   A by plane   B by ship   C by motorbike

8 If you were fearless, which of these would you be?

   A brave   B nervous   C anxious

4 Complete the text by choosing the correct word for each space.

Welcome to Kingslade Sports and Leisure Centre

As a new member of our centre, you 1............... be wondering how you existed 2............... Kingslade's range of sports and leisure activities. Your life has 3............... forever!

Perhaps you'd like to start each day with a 4............... swim? Or work out at lunchtimes in the gym? If so, let us 5............... you to stay on afterwards in our cafe, 6............... only the freshest and tastiest food is served.

It's important for you to look after yourself, and we're here to help you do just that, every day. Our quiet and peaceful 7............... is the first step to relaxation. Then, how about 8............... a break from the stress of daily living by making an appointment to have your back massaged in the health suite, or 9............... your hair restyled in the beauty room?

Make sure you 10............... everything that Kingslade has to offer you – soon!

1	A can	B must	C need	D ought
2	A without	B beyond	C by	D through
3	A developed	B cancelled	C banned	D changed
4	A long	B deep	C wide	D narrow
5	A insist	B persuade	C refuse	D agree
6	A what	B when	C where	D why
7	A location	B destination	C region	D situation
8	A putting	B doing	C taking	D holding
9	A give	B get	C keep	D be
10	A experiment	B imagine	C fetch	D try

Writing

5 Sort the sentences below into two messages by matching their content with questions A and B. Rewrite them on the postcards, adding suitable opening and closing formulae.

> Don't forget to mail me those copies of Newsweek you promised me!

> I'm sorry I haven't sent you any news for so long.

> How are your studies going – is engineering really hard?

> If you're free next summer, would you like to visit me at our beach house?

> My term finished last week, so I'm working in a supermarket to earn a bit of money.

> I know you love anything to do with art, so I decided to get this Matisse card for you.

A
You want to send a postcard to your Australian friend Vera.
In your postcard, you should

- apologise to Vera for not writing to her earlier
- explain why you have chosen this card for her
- invite Vera to come and stay next year.

B
You want to send a postcard to your penfriend in Canada.
In your postcard, you should

- ask your penfriend about her university course
- say what you are doing at the moment
- remind your penfriend to send you some magazines.

Dear ...

Dear ...

EXAM TASKS IN MODULE 5

Unit 17 – Paper 1 Reading Part 3
Unit 18 – Paper 3 Speaking Parts 3 and 4
Unit 19 – Paper 2 Listening Part 3
Unit 20 – Paper 1 Reading Part 1

Make sure you read the relevant parts of the Exam guide before doing these tasks.

Topics

1 What can you see in the photos? What topics do they show?

Vocabulary

2 For groups 1–4, say which noun is the odd one out and why. Then match the groups to three of the topics in **1**.

1 cheetah   lion   tiger   elephant
2 biology   chemistry   physics   science
3 dolphin   shark   sheep   whale
4 colleague   director   manager   staff

Grammar

3 Match sentences 1–3 to a grammar area a–c and underline the word(s) that show you this.

1 The wildlife photos in the exhibition were taken by a neighbour of ours.

2 Finn left school to get a job.

3 Julie tried acting, singing and dancing, but she was never going to be a success on the stage.

a a sentence expressing purpose
b a possessive structure
c a sentence using a gerund

17.2 All work and no play

Warm up

1 What negative aspects of work do the photos show?

2 Discuss the questions.

- How many hours a week do people work on average?/How many hours a week should people work on average?
- How many weeks' holiday do people have each year?/How many weeks' holiday should people have each year?
- At what age do people retire?/At what age should people retire?

Reading Part 3

→ **EXAM GUIDE** PAGE 110

3 Look at the sentences below about holidays and work.

Read the text to decide if each sentence is correct or incorrect.
If it is correct, mark A.
If it is not correct, mark B.

1 Nowadays, more than half of all Americans would prefer to decrease their time at work.
2 American companies give three weeks' holiday a year.
3 Joe Robinson first suggested his idea for a new law in a TV interview.
4 He thinks children should have longer holidays as well.
5 American couples work longer hours than they used to.
6 Mark Liechty thinks Europeans make clear differences between being at home and being at work.
7 It is thought that in the 19ᵗʰ century factory workers suffered from stress.
8 Only a small number of Americans are ill due to long working hours.
9 Robinson advises people to ask for longer holidays before they join a company.
10 If you work for an American company in Europe, you get longer holidays.

Work can damage your health

Americans work the most hours and get the shortest holidays in the developed world. They work, on average, two weeks longer a year than the second most overworked group in the world, the Japanese. A survey by the Families and Work Institute found out that 63 per cent of Americans want to work less, up from 46 per cent in 1992.

Joe Robinson, editor of *Escape* magazine, wrote a special report on the lack of holidays in the USA. He reminded readers that Western Europeans and Australians get five weeks' holiday a year compared to 9.6 days in the USA. He encouraged Americans to demand a new law which would give every worker who has been in a job for a year three weeks off, increasing to four weeks off after three years. The idea was immediately popular and since then, Robinson has appeared on TV and radio talk shows.

'Once people think about it more carefully, they find out it's not just about holidays,' explains Robinson. 'It's

about family values, having time for your kids. It's about your health and your relationships. It's about the quality of life.' He says the average husband and wife together spend 500 hours a year more at work than they did in 1980.

It isn't easy for Americans to take time off. Mark Liechty, a professor at University of Illinois, Chicago, says that Americans work hard in order to buy anything they want and to make themselves into the people they want to be. He feels Europeans are better at separating life and work. They understand the importance of having a life outside work.

The strongest argument for longer holidays is health. Research has found that in the late 19th century, people who worked with their brains (rather than, for example, factory workers), became 'nervous and anxious' because they needed time away from work. A recent study has shown that men who don't take holidays are both more likely to die young and to suffer from heart disease. It is thought that half of all Americans are damaging their health through overwork.

Until three-week holidays become law, Robinson encourages those looking for jobs to ask for more holiday time when they are discussing salary and benefits after accepting a job offer. 'It's the best opportunity to get the time you need.' He adds that American companies in Europe all give their employees European-length holidays. 'If they can do it there, why can't they do it here?' he asks. ' Tell your employer that you are going to work very hard, but at the same time, you need a holiday.'

Writing

4 Read the note and ideas about changes at work. In which two areas do the staff suggest changes?

> Kris
> Could you get some ideas from people in the office for any changes which would make our staff happier in their jobs? Can you write me a short note with a few recommendations?
> Many thanks
> Richard

Changes at work

I'd like to be able to work around the children's school times. At the moment, I have to leave my son and daughter at school 20 minutes before it opens. I could start work half an hour later and only take half an hour's lunch break.

Changes at work

Why can't we use the internet at lunchtimes? We work long hours here and I could order my shopping from the supermarket.

Is there any chance of finishing earlier on a Friday? We could work longer hours on Monday to Thursday, or have shorter lunch breaks. It would be great to finish at, say, 3 o'clock on Fridays.

I'd like to use email for personal messages, not all day, but during breaks. It won't cost the company very much.

5 Richard has asked Kris to write a short note. Look at how he makes his first point. Add one or two sentences about the second point. The whole note should not be longer than 45 words.

> Richard
> These are my recommendations from the staff's suggestions. Firstly, they would like to be able to choose their working hours.

6 Imagine you have to hand in a piece of work at the end of the week. Write a note to your teacher or lecturer asking for more time to complete it. Explain why you cannot hand it in on time, and tell him/her exactly when you will hand it in. Write 35–45 words.

> **EXAM TIP** In Writing Part 2 you only write between 35–45 words so the information you include needs to be short and clear.

18.1 Fame

Warm up

1 Discuss the questions.

- Why do people become famous? Make a list of five people who have become famous for different reasons.
- What are the advantages of being famous?
- What are the disadvantages of having a very public life?

Vocabulary

→ VOCABULARY REFERENCE PAGE 125

2 We can make compound adjectives by putting two adjectives together, or an adjective and a noun. Complete the headlines with the compound adjectives.

broken-hearted   year-long   world-famous

> 1 .... **fashion designer marries childhood sweetheart**

> 2 Soap star say she's .... at leaving the series after 8 years

> 3 **Pop idol tells the truth after a .... silence**

3 Complete the notices and headlines by choosing a word from each list to make compound adjectives.

well	minute
late	made
home	cold
ice	price
half	night
last	behaved

1 Sale! Jackets ....
2 New family restaurant opening – all our food is ....
3 .... drinks sold here – perfect to cool you down.
4 Home needed for .... dog.
5 Want to go away this weekend? Call us for plenty of .... bargain holidays.
6 Tindale Shopping Mall – open till 9p.m. for .... shopping on Thursdays.

Listening

4 You will hear a man talking about this film actress. Do you know who she is? Can you name any films she has appeared in? Listen and choose the correct answer for questions 1–6.

1 This actress's first acting role was
   A in a TV programme.
   B in a film.
   C in an advertisement.

2 The people who worked on ET
   A wanted her to believe that the ET doll was real.
   B thought she didn't like acting her character.
   C were worried because she was cold and hungry.

3 Drew handled her problems by
   A drinking a lot of coffee.
   B writing a book.
   C going on a diet.

4 The film, *Never been kissed*, was
   A the first film Drew produced and acted in.
   B her first success after her difficulties.
   C so good she made a second film in the series.

5 What part did Drew play in *Riding in cars with boys*?
   A her own mother
   B a woman she had known for nine years
   C a woman like her mother

6 Drew's plans for the future include
   A acting in films she already knows about.
   B making films with happy endings.
   C offering her story to a film company.

5 Listen again to check your answers. Then say why you have chosen those answers. Can you explain why the other options are wrong?

Example

1 C is the correct answer because we hear that her *first appearance on television … in an advert for dog food.* A is wrong because the radio presenter talks about *her first appearance on television*, not in a television programme. B is wrong because the film came after the advertisement.

Speaking
Parts 3 and 4

→ **EXAM GUIDE** PAGE 119

6 Work in pairs, Student A and Student B.

Part 3

* You are going to talk about photographs of people who are famous for different reasons.
* Student A: tell your partner what you can see in the first photo.
* Student B: tell your partner what you can see in the second photo.

Part 4

* The photos show people who are famous for different reasons.
  Which famous people do you most admire? Why?
  Would you like to be famous? What for?
  What would you enjoy and not enjoy about being famous?

18.2 Glittering prizes

Warm up

1 What 'measurements' of fame do the photos show? In what other ways do we recognise fame?

Grammar

Quantity

→ **GRAMMAR REFERENCE** PAGE 135

2 Add these phrases to the list below in the correct places.

a bit (of)   plenty (of)   a little   a number (of)
none

    no / not … any / ……………
    a few / …………… / ……………
    some
    several / ……………
    a lot (of) / lots (of) / ……………

3 Say whether the underlined nouns in sentences 1–4 are countable or uncountable. Then complete them with *a little, any, no, a few*.

1 I'm sorry. I've got …………… <u>coffee</u>. You'll have to have tea.
2 There were only …………… <u>people</u> in the audience last night – under 20, I'd say.
3 Clare hadn't won …………… <u>prizes</u> before she went to college.
4 …………… <u>luck</u> at the beginning of your career is a good thing.

4 Are the quantity words and phrases in **2** used with countable or uncountable nouns, or both?

5 Read the examples and rule and complete the text using words made from *some, any, no, every* with *-one, -body, -thing, -where*.

Everybody knows that getting an Oscar is the greatest achievement for a film actor.
There is nowhere more glamorous than Hollywood.
We can join *some, any, no* and *every* with *-one / -body, -thing* and *-where* to make words to refer to people, things and places.

---

1 ………… you ever wanted to know about the Oscars

• **Where do the stars receive their Oscars?**
The Academy Awards Ceremony takes place **2** …………… in Los Angeles, usually in one of the two biggest theatres.

• **Why are the results in envelopes?**
In the early years of the Oscars the results were given to the newspapers so that they could publish them at 11p.m. on the night of the ceremony. In 1940, however, guests arriving for the ceremony were able to buy the 8.45p.m. edition of the Los Angeles Times, which announced the results, so **3** …………… knew the winners in advance. The following year the 'sealed envelope' system was introduced and the results were no longer given to the newspapers early, so now, **4** …………… knows the winners beforehand.

• **Has 5 …………… ever been nominated more than once in the same year?**
Yes, a few times **6** …………… has been nominated for Leading Actor / Actress and Best Supporting Actor / Actress in the same year, Sigourney Weaver and Emma Thompson, for example.

Reading

6 Do you know what famous prize-giving ceremony the photo shows? What do you know about it? These words may give you a clue.

Physics   Chemistry   Medicine   Literature   Peace

7 Complete the text by choosing the correct word for each space.

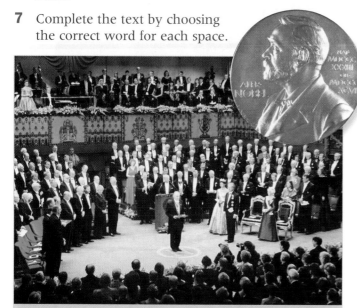

Every year in Stockholm on 10 December there is an event which is famous throughout the world. It is the Nobel Prize-giving Ceremony. This is a very special day 1 .... prizes are given to scientists, artists and peace-makers who have 2 .... more of a difference than anyone else in their subject.

The event has grown enormously 3 .... 1901 when only 150 guests (4 .... male) attended. Now, around 1,800 people, including the Nobel Prize winners who are 5 .... alive, are invited. It is a day of fun and luxury. The winners 6 .... their prizes from the Swedish King. The prize-giving is followed by an enormous celebration dinner in the Town Hall.

The 7 .... reason it is so popular is that the Nobel prizes have 8 .... a special place in society. Many 9 .... international prizes exist, but 10 .... of them are so well respected.

1	A which	B why	C when	D that
2	A made	B done	C had	D got
3	A in	B by	C after	D since
4	A each	B every	C all	D no
5	A yet	B still	C already	D ever
6	A fetch	B pick	C receive	D handle
7	A big	B best	C top	D main
8	A created	B earned	C reached	D become
9	A similar	B same	C near	D likely
10	A neither	B any	C none	D some

Writing

8 Read the task and Sara's answer. Find pairs of phrases or sentences in which she gives the same information.

> In your next letter tell me about someone who has influenced you. How do you know this person? How has he/she influenced you?

Dear Eric

It was good to hear from you. You asked me to tell you about someone who has influenced me. I'm going to tell you about someone. He is my history lecturer. He teaches at my university and he has influenced me a lot. When he teaches us he asks us to pretend we are the people in history, and say what we would do if we were in their situation. We try not to know what we know now, but try to think like they did in the past. You can understand more about history when you think like this. It really works. It has made me understand today's world better. I can understand people more now, if I try to think like them.

Yours,

Sara

9 Rewrite Sara's letter in your own words. Write one or two sentences for each question in the task.

10 You are going to write a letter to a friend about someone who has influenced you. First make some notes about the person and how they have influenced you using these questions to help.

Who?
Where did you meet? / Have you met?
In what way(s) has this person changed you?
Have you changed your life as a result?
Write your letter in about 100 words.

EXAM TIP Try to vary the words and phrases you use in your writing and check you have not repeated the same ideas.

19.1 In captivity

Warm up

1 Do you enjoy watching TV documentaries about the natural world? Have you ever been to a zoo? If so, did you enjoy your visit? Why / Why not?

Reading

2 Read A–D and match them to these text types.

article title   letter   speech   diary entry

A

> I'm enclosing $20. What you're doing sounds really important and I'm looking forward to finding out more at your next event.

B

> **Why many zoos still have a useful purpose**

C

> 25 FRIDAY
> We were at the zoo for over three hours today. I liked the monkeys best and so did my friend! They seemed to be really enjoying themselves.

D

> Some people argue that zoos have a conservation role now, but how can such stressed, unhealthy animals be useful to science?

3 Read the short texts 1–3 and decide which of A–D in **2** they are connected to. Think about the focus and meaning of each one.

4 Find words and phrases in the texts that mean the same as 1–5. The text number is in brackets.

1 (animals) at risk (1)
2 meaningless life (2)
3 not much chance of (2)
4 nothing is known about where they come from (3)
5 (keeping animals to) produce young (3)

1	2	3
Species Survival Plans (SSPs), managed by the American Zoo and Aquarium Association (AZA), already operate for certain animals. The purpose of these programs is to support, rather than replace, wild populations. It is essential to keep healthy examples of endangered animals in zoos, for the long-term survival of their species. In the future, their genetic material could be used either to recreate lost populations or to make animals in the wild stronger, so that they will continue to exist.	Zoos teach people that it is acceptable to keep animals locked up, bored, lonely, and far from their natural homes. Virginia McKenna, star of the classic movie *Born Free* about Elsa the lion, says: 'It is the sadness of zoos which particularly upsets me. The purposeless existence of the animals. For the four hours we spend in a zoo, the animals spend four years, or fourteen, perhaps even longer, day and night, summer and winter. This is not conservation and surely it is not education. No, it is "entertainment". Not comedy, however, but tragedy.' A worldwide study of zoos by the Born Free Foundation has shown that 'zoochosis' – strange and unnatural behaviour – is common in zoo animals. Stressed by their environment and with little opportunity for physical exercise, they do unusual things like biting the bars of their cages, or indeed, their own bodies.	At the Feline Conservation Center, Project Tiger is going well and we've already built the pools for Caesar and Jasmine. Both of these tigers are of unknown background, so will not be bred, but we still plan to bring in Sumatran tigers for breeding when Project Tiger is finished. Our Summer Tour will take place on June 22 and anyone who has given money to FCC is welcome to join in the fun. A big thank-you to those of you who have helped us in other ways recently: to David and Adrianne for their 'old' computer equipment, to Brent and Vicki for the 1999 Nissan truck, and to American Data Plates, who continue to print this newsletter for us. We receive no public money, so really need your help to save and protect the world's big cats.

5 Read sentences 1–5 and say whether they are correct or incorrect.

1 The AZA makes sure that healthy animals from zoos are returned to the wild.
2 Virginia McKenna once appeared in a film about a lion.
3 Animals in zoos develop habits that wild animals don't have.
4 The tigers Caesar and Jasmine are going to produce tiger cubs.
5 The Feline Conservation Center depends on its supporters for financial help.

Grammar

So / neither / nor

→ **GRAMMAR REFERENCE** PAGE 135

6 In a discussion, you can agree with someone by using short phrases with *so* or *nor/neither*. Read the examples and complete the rules with *so* or *neither*.

I think zoos should be closed. > *So do I.*
I haven't been to a zoo recently. > *Neither/Nor have I.*

If the verb used is in the affirmative, you answer with ....
If the verb used is in the negative, you answer with ....

7 In pairs, read statements 1–8 about zoos and say whether you agree with them or not. If you aren't sure, say so.

You say	Your partner agrees with you	Your partner disagrees with you
I agree.	*So do I.*	*I don't.*
I don't agree.	*Neither / Nor do I.*	*I do.*
I'm not sure.	*Nor / Neither am I.*	*I am.*

1 Zoos had a more important educational role 100 years ago than they do nowadays.
2 Nowadays, with television and the internet, zoos are no longer necessary.
3 Zoos are still important, but their role has changed from education to conservation.
4 Most zoos look after their animals well.
5 It is unfair to keep animals in zoos, away from their natural environment.
6 Many zoo animals are born in captivity, so they don't miss the wild.
7 Zoo animals often suffer stress.
8 Without zoos, some animals could disappear altogether.

8 Complete the second sentence of each pair so that it means the same as the first, using *so*, *neither* or *nor*.

1 People used to kill tigers and leopards for their fur.
Tigers used to be killed for their fur and .... leopards.
2 Lions and most other big cats don't like swimming.
Lions don't like swimming and .... most other big cats.
3 Tigers and jaguars, however, will happily enter water.
However, tigers will happily enter water and .... jaguars.
4 Leopards can live in hot tropical forests or on cold mountains.
Hot tropical forests are home to leopards and .... cold mountains.
5 Lions and tigers aren't as fast as cheetahs.
Lions aren't as fast as cheetahs and .... tigers.

Speaking

9 Discuss your views on the role of zoos today. Choose one of the questions to start your discussion and continue with the other questions. Use the ideas in the texts in **3** to help you.

Do you really think zoos help to save endangered animals?

But how acceptable is it to keep animals locked up, in your view?

What do you personally like or dislike about visiting a zoo?

So what conclusions have we reached together?

19.2 In the wild

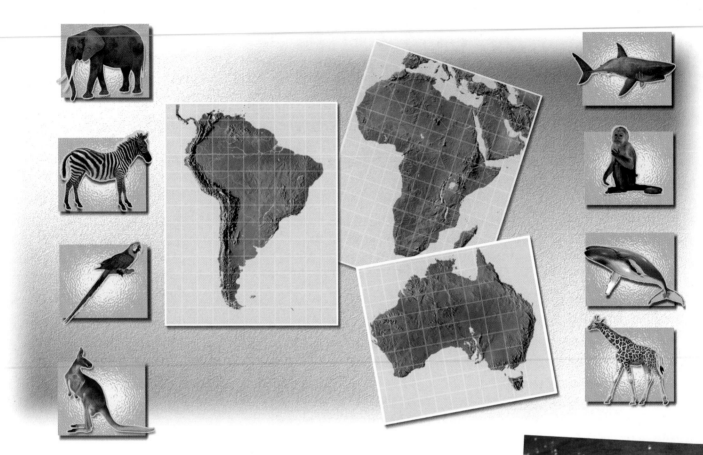

Warm up

→ VOCABULARY REFERENCE PAGE 125

1 What names of wild animals and birds do you know in English? Match the pictures to these words and say which part of the world each animal or bird lives in. What other wild animals do you know from each place?

elephant   giraffe   kangaroo
monkey   parrot   shark
whale   zebra

2 Which of these would offer the best opportunities to see wildlife? Which would you prefer to do and why?

* a balloon trip over African grassland
* a trek through the Brazilian rainforest
* a week's diving on the Great Barrier Reef

Listening Part 3

→ EXAM GUIDE PAGE 116

3 You will hear a woman talking to a group of students about a diving trip. For each question, fill in the missing information in the numbered space.

DIVING ON THE GREAT BARRIER REEF, AUSTRALIA

COMPANY: UNDERSEA EXPLORER
   Why company is unusual – carries out (1) ....

ON BOARD:
   Cabins for two with (2) ....
   Who else takes part – a couple of (3) ....

TRAINING COURSE:
   Essential unless person has dived within (4) .... months.

UNDERWATER WILDLIFE ON OSPREY REEF EXPEDITION:
   Speaker saw a variety of (5) ....

WHEN TRIPS ARE AVAILABLE:
   Every month apart from (6) ....

Vocabulary

4 Read the example and make phrases from the verbs and the prepositions. Sometimes more than one preposition is possible.

Undersea Explorer *insist on* people doing a training course if they haven't dived recently.

advise apologise believe	for
blame check decide hope	against
involve protect spend warn	on
	in

Writing

5 Complete the story with some of the verbs and prepositions in **4**. How do you think it should end? What do you think happened to Charlie?

An African experience

I'll never forget Charlie. I met him in Tanzania, where we were 1 .... a rhino conservation project. We both 2 .... what we were doing, and wanted to stay on in Africa. Fortunately (or unfortunately, in Charlie's case) we were offered new conservation jobs in either Kenya or Namibia and we both 3 .... Kenya. For this project, we drove long distances to 4 .... zebra populations, camping in the wild at night. It was wonderful being out under the stars, but with lions in the area, it was also dangerous. The project leaders had 5 .... us .... sleeping outside, but Charlie didn't listen.

6 Read endings 1–3. In your opinion, which is the best and why? Which is the least successful and why?

1
> One night, he went off for a walk on his own. I tried to persuade him not to go but it was useless. They found his water bottle a couple of days later.

2
> The night it happened, I was sleeping in the 4-wheel drive. Charlie's screams woke me up. I switched on the headlights and the lion ran off, but Charlie had lost too much blood. He died in my arms.

3
> He slept on a mat every night and used to wake me in the morning with a mug of tea.

EXAM TIP In the Writing Part 3 Story, make sure your story reaches a definite ending.

7 Read the exam task and plan your story by working through questions 1-8. Then write your story in about 100 words.

- Your English teacher has asked you to write a story.

- Your story must begin with the following sentence:

  Ben and Sam realised that they were lost in the forest.

1 Why did Ben and Sam realise they were lost?
2 Where exactly were they?
3 What time of day was it?
4 How did they feel? (Worried? Angry?) Why?
5 What did they decide to do? (Shout for help? Light a fire?)
6 How long were they in the forest for?
7 Did they find their own way out or did someone help them?
8 How did they feel at the end of this experience?

20.1 Get ready!

Warm up

1 Read the advice on exam preparation and decide when it would be best to carry out each piece of advice. What advice would you add? Why?

two weeks before   five days before   the day before

EXAM COUNTDOWN

3
- ▶ Check exactly when and where the exam will take place.
- ▶ Get to bed at a reasonable time and set your alarm clock.
- ▶ Prepare a checklist of the things you need to revise.

2
- ▶ Spend some time relaxing and eat and drink what you particularly enjoy.
- ▶ Work through some timed practice questions.

1
- ▶ Don't try to learn anything new now – it might damage your confidence.

0
- ▶ Review the areas you have learned, to work out your strengths and weaknesses.

Speaking

2 Which things in the pictures aren't you allowed to have with you inside an exam room? Explain why you think these things are banned.

3 Choose one permitted thing and explain why you would like to have it with you on the exam day.

4 Do you believe objects can bring you luck? Why / Why not?

Reading Part 1

→ EXAM GUIDE PAGE 109

5 Look at the text in each question.
What does it say?
Mark the correct letter – A, B or C.

1

Carla
Could I borrow that new
book of yours overnight? I
need to check some facts
in my essay before handing
it in tomorrow. Thanks,
Mark

Mark wants Carla to
A look at an essay of his before
tomorrow.
B tell him the correct answers
later today.
C lend him something until
tomorrow.

2

**Silence in this area
please!**

**Candidates' interviews
are now in progress**

A You must be quiet here because
interviews are taking place.
B Candidates are requested to
wait in the silent area.
C We will tell you the result of
your interview later.

3

THURSDAY'S ITALIAN CINEMA EVENT

Talk on director Nanni Moretti's
work, followed by the film:
La stanza del figlio (The Son's
Room).

Open to all department
members and their guests

A The film will be shown after
Nanni Moretti's talk on
Thursday.
B Thursday's audience will
include people from outside the
department.
C This Thursday, the department
will be open until the film is
shown.

4

Travel grants

To: Geography students
From: Dr James's secretary

Anyone wishing to be considered
for a grant must first discuss
their application with Dr James in
person.

Geography students wanting a
grant should
A apply in writing for one
immediately.
B decide where to travel to first
of all.
C see Dr James himself before
they apply.

5

*Calming
Cranberry*

Nature's own recipe for
reducing stress
Pour boiling water onto
teabag and relax!

Why would people drink this tea?
A to keep themselves awake
B to make them less anxious
C to help them lose weight

Grammar

Possessive forms

→ GRAMMAR REFERENCE PAGE 135

6 Say what the examples have in
common and complete the rules
with *s*, *'s*, or *'* only.

*that new book of yours
candidates' interviews
Nanni Moretti's work
Dr James's students*

Genitive forms show belonging or
possession.

· For singular nouns, plurals and
names not ending in *s*, you add
....
· For plurals ending in *s*, you just add
....
· For names already ending in *s*, you
can add .... or just *'*.

*Sam's books were on the table and so
were* <u>mine</u>.

The pronouns *mine, yours, his, hers,
ours, theirs* also show possession.

an idea of hers, a student of ours

These possessive pronouns are
sometimes used in phrases with *of*.

7 Rewrite phrases 1–6 as genitive
forms.

Example
the registration form of the college
the college's registration form

1 the views of several women
2 the plays of Shakespeare
3 the members of the United
Nations
4 the qualifications of the
lecturers
5 the file belonging to Enrico
6 the daughter of Mr and Mrs
Jones

8 Complete sentences 1–4 by adding
a suitable possessive pronoun.

1 John came to the party with a
cousin of ....
2 We heard the news from an old
teacher of ....
3 Erica and Sally went to London
with a friend of ....
4 Have you ever met Karen?
She's an old friend of ....
from school.

20.2 Aim high!

Warm up

→ **VOCABULARY REFERENCE** PAGE 125

1 Is it still important for you to study? What qualifications do you already have? What subjects do you plan to continue? Which career are you aiming for?

Listening

2 You will hear a conversation between a boy, Daniel, and his mother, about his plans for university. Before you listen, read sentences 1–6 and match meanings a–f to the underlined verbs.

1 Daniel's careers teacher <u>has persuaded</u> Daniel to apply to university.
2 Daniel's mother <u>encourages</u> him to believe in his ability at school.
3 Daniel <u>intends</u> to study maths at university.
4 Daniel <u>agrees</u> that his recent work has been careless.
5 Daniel's mother <u>insists</u> that he should give up playing in the band.
6 Daniel <u>refuses</u> to make an appointment with the careers teacher.

a say that you won't do something
b want and plan to do something
c speak firmly about something
d have the same opinion as someone else
e talk someone into doing something
f make someone feel more confident

3 Listen and decide if sentences 1–6 are correct or incorrect.

Vocabulary

→ **VOCABULARY REFERENCE** PAGE 125

4 Match the phrases in sentences 1–5 to meanings a–e.

1 The angry child *paid no attention* to what her teacher was trying to tell her.
2 Steve's over there but I can't *attract his attention* – I'll have to shout at him!
3 Tell me what's wrong – I can *give you my full attention* for at least an hour.
4 Why did Sarah *pay so little attention* to her studies?
5 There's only a month left, so you must *turn your attention* to exam practice!

a listen carefully
b start concentrating on
c ignored completely
d spend minimum time on
e get someone to notice you

5 Read the examples and say what part of speech is formed when *-ation* or *-ment* is added to a verb.

He handed out lots of *information* to friends of mine. I'll make an *appointment* with the head of year instead.

6 Make nouns with *-ation* or *-ment* from the verbs and use them to complete sentences 1–6.

educate   encourage   explain
manage   organise   register

1 Unless you can give me a good .... for why you are so late, I'll have to report you to the Head.
2 Time .... is a very important skill to learn in the workplace.
3 At .... , please give us a passport-sized photo of yourself, for your college identity card.
4 UCAS is a central .... that handles all university applications in Britain.
5 Many people believe that standards of .... are falling, but recent exam results seem to show the opposite.
6 I've always received lots of .... and support from my family.

Writing

7 How can you score maximum marks in your writing? Read sentences 1–11 and decide whether they are correct or incorrect.
1 You will have 90 minutes for the whole of Paper 1, so manage your time carefully.
2 You must answer both the story and the letter questions in Part 3.
3 It is best to write a full rough answer to each question first.
4 You should use a wide range of grammar and vocabulary.
5 It doesn't matter if you write fewer words than the question asks for in Part 2.
6 In Part 3, you will lose marks if you write more words than the question asks for.
7 Remember to give all the information the question asks for.
8 You should start your sentences in a variety of ways, to avoid repeating yourself.
9 It is necessary to copy out the sentence or title in the story question.
10 You must write in pen on the answer sheet.
11 You will be given extra time to check your answers.

8 Using the true information in **7**, decide which answer to the task would get a higher mark, a or b.

• This is part of a letter you receive from your English friend Jo.

> My parents say I should apply for a job as soon as I finish at university, but I want to spend some time travelling first. How can I persuade them that my idea is best? What would you advise me to do?

• Write a letter answering Jo's questions.

a
Dear Jo
Thanks for your letter. I agree that your idea is best. You can apply for a job in a year's time!
Why don't you come and stay with me as soon as you finish university? Why don't I find you a job in my uncle's restaurant and then we could go travelling together later in the year. It's a good idea of mine, isn't it? Why don't you buy your plane ticket now?
Love Theo

b
Hi Jo
You've asked me for some advice about your problem. I think the most important thing is to make your parents believe in your idea, so why not spend some time explaining your plans to them. Show them a few maps and get them interested in the places you want to visit. If they realise you're properly prepared, I'm sure they'll agree with you in the end.
If I were you, I'd do the same thing, although personally, I'd want to earn some money first before travelling. Couldn't you get a summer job after university and then go off on your trip later in the year?
Keep in touch and send me lots of postcards!
Good luck
Maya

Grammar

1 Complete the second sentence of each pair so that it means the same as the first, using no more than three words.

   1 Jane and her sister both went to university in Edinburgh.
     Jane went to university in Edinburgh and .... her sister.
   2 Young pop stars need some luck as well as talent.
     As well as talent, young pop stars need a .... luck.
   3 Tammy wondered if the lion would escape if she opened his cage.
     Tammy opened the cage .... if the lion would escape.
   4 Primary and secondary schools don't teach sports nowadays.
     Primary schools don't teach sports nowadays, and .... secondary schools.
   5 Dr Hahn won several prizes for his scientific discoveries.
     Dr Hahn won a .... of prizes for his scientific discoveries.
   6 The star of the film expected an Oscar for her performance.
     The star of the film hoped .... an Oscar for her performance.
   7 The location of the conference this year is northern Italy.
     This year's conference is .... in northern Italy.
   8 Kathy told me why I should give money to the conservation project.
     Kathy tried to persuade .... give money to the conservation project.
   9 It was the most beautiful place I'd ever seen.
     I had never seen .... as beautiful.
  10 One of my colleagues at Kraft Foods has just become our director.
     The new director was a colleague of .... at Kraft Foods.

2 Choose the correct word for 1–8.

   1 My new boyfriend has promised to take me *anywhere / somewhere* romantic for my birthday.
   2 The new secretary *offered / suggested* to stay late and help prepare for the conference.
   3 Mrs Shaw doesn't want me to study conservation and *so / neither* do my parents.
   4 We met Tom and Carol in town with a friend of *ours / theirs* we hadn't met before.
   5 There were *a lot / several* of applicants for the job, but only *a few / none* of them had any experience.
   6 There's *anyone / no one* better qualified for the job than Mike Smith.
   7 If you do a *little / few* English homework every day, you'll do well in the exam.
   8 I was shocked by the condition of the *animal's / animals'* cages.

Vocabulary

3 Complete the compound adjectives in 1–5.

1 Gail was broken-.............. when she didn't get the job.

2 I couldn't believe I found myself sitting next to a world- .... actor on the plane.

3 It was a last- .... decision to go to Africa to help on the conservation project, but I didn't regret it.

4 There's a sale on at the department store – some of the clothes are half-............... .

5 Some people think late- .... studying helps them to prepare for an exam the next day.

4 Complete 1–5 with a verb in the correct tense.

agree   insist   intend   persuade   refuse

1 Jill .... her boss to give her a pay rise last week.

2 Kevin .... to study for another degree when he graduates later this year – he wants to be a university lecturer.

3 Lola .... to re-take the exam she failed – she's already thrown away all her books.

4 Max .... that he didn't copy his essay from a website.

5 Jonny and I have spoken about the importance of getting good marks and he .... to study harder for his exams.

5 Complete the newspaper extracts with a suitable verb in the correct tense.

In its meeting on Wednesday the council 1.............. against closing the zoo because it believes the zoo provides an educational service. In a short statement, they 2.............. protesters that if they caused trouble they would have them arrested. The council also said that it would do everything possible to look after and 3.............. the animals against anyone who tried to set them free.

There was more trouble at Twineham Zoo last night. Zoo Manager, Mica Bedloe, said, 'I 4.............. for signs of disturbance before I left work yesterday and everything was fine, but this morning I saw that cages had been damaged. I 5.............. the protesters for this. The zoo will be closed this week while we repair the damage. We 6.............. for any inconvenience this causes to school visits.'

6 Write nouns ending in -*ment* or -*ation* next to definitions 1–5.

1 when you give a reason for something ....

2 when you have a paid job ....

3 a group of people who make a business or club together ....

4 the teaching or training or people, especially in schools ....

5 when you give support or confidence to somebody ....

Writing

7 Read the task, then decide which three of 1–7 answer it in 45 words or less. Remember to answer the question and avoid repeating information.

You want to help a conservation project.

Write a note to your friends. In your note, you should

- explain why you are writing to them

- tell them about the project

- encourage them to give money to the project.

1 How are you? I've got a new job. I'm working with the Animal Conservation Project. It's really interesting and I might have the opportunity to go to Africa.

2 If you want to help, send £5 to the Animal Support Organisation.

3 All around the world animals which are in danger are being killed so that their fur can be made into things for people to buy, like shoes and coats. This is still happening even though there are laws against it.

4 I'm writing to ask you to support an important conservation project.

5 We need to get lots of people involved. Our local newspaper has agreed to write an article and ask readers to send money to support the project.

6 Please help to tell everyone about the Animal Support Organisation and ask them to send £5. I hope you will give them £5 too.

7 Hundreds of endangered animals are still being killed for their fur despite laws and serious punishment for anyone caught.

8 Read the first part of this story, then write the rest of it by answering the questions below.

I used to work for quite a big insurance company. One week, when I came to work in the mornings, I was sure someone else had used my desk and computer since I'd left the night before. It didn't happen the next week and I forgot all about it. Then I started getting some strange emails. They were written to me and whoever wrote them knew all about me. The sender called himself Gerry and he would ask me how I was, and then mention things I had done in the past few days. I didn't reply but got more and more angry and upset. Then I suddenly knew what to do.

- Did the writer reply to the emailer or take another course of action?
- Did the emails stop or increase?
- Did the writer meet the emailer or speak to them on the phone?
- Who was the emailer?

Additional materials

6.1

Listening

Exercise 7

1 A 4km
   B 42km
   C 180km

2 A He trained by walking up and down stairs.
   B He found out he could win long-distance races.
   C He continued to practise running bigger distances.

3 A He concentrates on the finish of the race.
   B He thinks about each part of the race separately.
   C He knows he can continue unless he is unwell.

4 A He explains how hard work leads to success.
   B He encourages them to enter competitions.
   C He tells them not to give up.

7.2

Listening

Exercise 8

W Dan, I'm definitely going to enter the Gordon Ramsay cooking competition. The top prize is £5,000!

M Are you sure you're old enough? Don't the rules say you can't enter unless you're between 18 and 25?

W Yes, but that's on the first of July this year and my birthday's two weeks before, so I just qualify.

M Oh, that's OK then. But what about the people at work. Are they happy for you to take part? You haven't been there very long…

W Actually, it was the head chef who told me to find out about it. He thinks it'd be good training for me, says it would make me think about recipes a bit more and, you know, find my own style.

M Sounds sensible. So, any ideas about what to prepare?

W Well, it has to be a three-course lunch, which includes oysters in one or more of the courses.

M Oysters! You can use them raw or cooked, I suppose. I can't imagine eating something fishy like that in a dessert, though!

W Mmm, I admit it's unlikely, although this is a competition, so the recipes should be unusual. I think I'll experiment a little…

M Well, don't try any oyster desserts on me! (*Disgusted*) Ugh, makes me feel sick…

W Dan, you're not exactly being helpful, are you!

M Oh Kelly, you know I'm only joking. You're a brilliant chef, honestly.

W Really?

M Yeah. Look, what else do you have to do apart from the menu?

W Well, it says here write a 250-word essay, giving professional aims for the future.

M You'll never be able to keep to the word length!

W Very amusing… you're right, though. I mean, I could talk about my dream of having a vegetarian café … and that idea I had recently for a book of recipes, and …

M Yes yes, but be careful to give enough detail and make it sound as though one thing follows from the other…

W Like, if I manage to open the café, I'll try to publish the recipes that I use there. Yes, it sounds better linked together. I'm starting to feel that prize has already got my name on it!

M Maybe. Come on then, Kelly, where can we buy oysters round here?

16.1

Speaking Part 1 Exam Task

Exercise 4

Student A

You are the examiner. Introduce yourself and ask Student B these questions.

Student A   I'm ....
            What's your name?

Student B   ....

Student A   What's your surname?

Student B   ....

Student A   How do you spell it?

Student B   ....

Student A   Where do you come from?

Student B   ....

Student A   Do you enjoy studying English? Why (not)?

Student B   ....

Now you are the candidate. Answer the questions the examiner (Student B) asks you.

12.1

Listening

Exercise 7

M Lorna, why did you have to see the boss in his office just now?

W Oh, Sam, there's no point talking about it…

M Come on, you can share your problem with me, Lorna. It can't be as bad as all that – you're one of the best employees here.

W (*Pause*) I was, you mean…

M Hey, what's happened?

W OK, I'll tell you. You see, I had a stupid argument with my best friend last night. I was really unpleasant to her and I wanted to apologise this morning, but she wasn't answering her mobile…

M So you sent her an email from work, which we're not allowed to do.

W How did you guess? I'd never done anything wrong here until today. And it's such an unfair rule anyway…

M You're right of course, but I think you have to accept the way things are here and get on with your job. I mean you can't change anything, can you?

W Maybe. Anyway, it's too late now.

M How do you mean? They can't tell you to leave just like that. As your boss, David would have to explain the problem in writing first and then …

W Yeah, I know all that, but the thing is, I got really angry with David and… well, I told him what he could do with this job!

M Ah… (*Laughs*) You always say what's on your mind, don't you! I suppose that was the problem last night too?

W Exactly. I opened my big mouth and then felt awful afterwards. Mind you, I'm glad I spoke to David like that. It gave him a nasty shock!

M Well, whatever you said it shouldn't cost you your job. Look, do you want me to speak to him? I'm sure he won't want to lose you.

W It's OK, really, but thanks for offering.

M Well, it <u>is</u> up to you – I was only trying to help.

W I suppose I just have to wait and see what happens now.

16.1

Speaking Part 1 Exam Task

Exercise 4

Student B

You are the candidate. Answer the questions the examiner (Student A) asks you.

Now you are the examiner. Introduce yourself and ask Student A these questions.

Student B I'm ....
What's your name?

Student A ....

Student B What's your surname?

Student A ....

Student B How do you spell it?

Student A ....

Student B Do you work or are you a student?

Student A ....

Student B What do you enjoy doing in your free time?

Student A ....

3.1

Vocabulary

Exercise 1

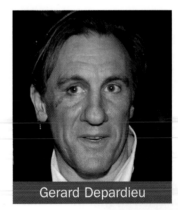
Gerard Depardieu

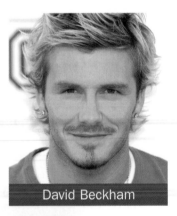
David Beckham

Kate Winslet

PET Exam guide

 Reading Part 1

Notices and messages

Facts

- Part 1 contains five multiple-choice questions (1–5) and an example.
- You must choose one of three explanations – A, B or C.
- The questions test your understanding of five short texts.
- The five texts include public notices and personal messages such as emails, handwritten notes and postcards.
- You are usually shown where the text is – for example, in a shop window, on a computer screen.

Technique

▼ Read the text carefully and think about its purpose.
▼ Read the three explanations and mark your choice of answer in pencil.
▼ Decide why the other two explanations are wrong.
▼ Check that your choice of answer has the same meaning as the text.
▼ Mark your final choice – A, B or C – on the answer sheet.

Tips

- Wrong answers often contain the same words as the text. Think about how these words are used in both the text and the explanations.
- Notices often say what you can and mustn't do. Revise uses of modal verbs before the exam.
- Personal messages may include different names. Decide on the relationships between these people and remember who is writing to who.

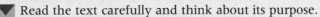

TRAINING FOR READING PART 1 IN *PET MASTERCLASS*
NOTICES: 2.1; MESSAGES: 12.1, 16.1; EXAM TASK: 20.1

 Reading Part 2

Matching people to short texts

Facts

- Part 2 contains five descriptions (6–10) and eight short texts (A–H).
- Each short description is about a person or people (usually a family or a group of friends).
- The eight texts contain information on, for example, different types of accommodation, books, holidays, museums, websites.
- You must choose the most suitable accommodation, book, holiday, etc. for each person or people.
- The correct choice must include **all** the personal requirements in the description.

Technique

▼ Read the instructions to find out the topic of the eight texts.

▼ Read each description and circle any personal 'limits' – for example, only free on Wednesdays/at weekends/after 5p.m., not much money to spend, in the city centre, doesn't have a car.

▼ Underline other key words in the description that show personal requirements.

▼ Scan the eight texts, rejecting any that are outside the limits.

▼ Concentrate on the remaining texts (probably a maximum of three), reading each one carefully for the requirements.

▼ When you think you've found the right text, check it once more against the description.

▼ Move on to the next description and repeat the same steps as above.

▼ Check at the end that all your answers are different letters.

▼ Mark your choices – A–H – on the answer sheet.

Tips

• Don't waste time reading all eight texts through at the beginning – the descriptions will tell you what information to scan for.

• When you decide on an answer, read the chosen text carefully; finding the same words in the description and text doesn't mean a correct answer!

• Make sure that every element of the description is included in the text you think is correct.

• Check you have shaded the right box on the answer sheet.

TRAINING FOR READING PART 2 IN *PET MASTERCLASS*
3.2, 6.2, 9.1; EXAM TASK: 15.2

Reading Part 3

True / false sentences about a long text

Facts

• Part 3 contains ten sentences (11–20) and a long text.

• You have to decide whether each sentence is correct (A) or incorrect (B).

• The text and questions focus on facts or information.

• The sentences about the text are in the same order as the information in the text.

• There are no 'negative' sentences – for example, you will never see a sentence containing the word 'not'.

Technique

▼ Read the instructions to find out what the topic of the text is.

▼ Read the ten sentences and then read the text quickly to get a general idea of the content.

▼ Read the first sentence and underline the key words.

▼ Look for similar information in the text and highlight it.

▼ Read the sentence and highlighted text again and decide whether the sentence is correct or incorrect.

▼ Write A (correct) or B (incorrect) against the question number.

▼ Transfer your answers to the answer sheet when you have completed all ten sentences.

Tips

- Think of the different ways of saying something – you are very unlikely to find the same words used in both the sentence and the text.
- As you work through the sentences, mark each number against the text, so that you know where to start looking for the answer to the next sentence.
- Don't worry if there are words you don't understand in the text – they will not be tested.
- Don't guess about a sentence unless you get really stuck – you need to read the text to find the answer.

TRAINING FOR READING PART 3 IN *PET MASTERCLASS*
1.1, 8.1, 11.1, EXAM TASK: 17.2, 19.1

Reading Part 4

Opinion text with multiple-choice questions

Facts

- Part 4 contains a text and five multiple-choice questions (21–25).
- The questions have four options – A, B, C or D.
- This part of the test needs slow, careful reading of both the text and the questions.
- The text will usually focus on the writer's attitude or opinion.
- The questions test different things – for example, Question 21 is about the writer's purpose in writing the text, Question 25 is about the overall meaning.
- Questions 22–24 are in the order of the text.

Technique

▼ Read the text twice: once to get a general idea of content and a second time to get a more detailed understanding.
▼ Try to answer Questions 21 and 25 first.
▼ Then work through Questions 22–24, checking your choice of answers against the text.
▼ Go back to Questions 21 and 25 and check your first answers are correct.
▼ Mark your answers – A, B, C or D – on the answer sheet.

Part 4

| 0 | A | | C | D |

Tips

- Read the text and questions very carefully, so that you don't misunderstand anything.
- Wrong answers often contain the same words as the text. Think about how these words are used in both the text and the questions.

TRAINING FOR READING PART 4 IN *PET MASTERCLASS*
5.1, 7.1, 19.1; EXAM TASK: 13.1

Reading Part 5

Short text testing vocabulary and grammar

Facts

- Part 5 consists of a short text and ten multiple-choice questions (26–35).
- You must choose one of four options – A, B, C or D.
- The questions test mainly vocabulary and some grammar.
- The texts are usually factual.

Technique

▼ Read the text once for meaning, not thinking about the spaces.
▼ Look through the questions before you read the text again.
▼ Decide on each answer, circling the letter.
▼ Read the text again with your answers in place to check it makes sense.
▼ Mark your answers – A, B, C or D – on the answer sheet.

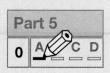

Part 5

| 0 | A | | C | D |

- Check that your answers agree with the words around the space – for example, look out for pronouns before a space and prepositions after one.
- Think about the meaning of the whole sentence as you decide on an answer.
- For questions that test vocabulary, the other words may be similar in meaning, so you need to decide why they are wrong.
- For questions that test grammar, check agreement, tense, or number earlier in the sentence or in the sentence before.

TRAINING FOR READING PART 5 IN *PET MASTERCLASS*
4.1, 8.2, 14.1, 18.2; ALL MODULE REVIEWS; EXAM TASK: 10.1

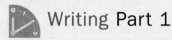 Writing Part 1

Transformations

Facts

- This Part consists of five questions (1–5) and an example.
- All the questions are about the same topic.
- Each question gives a whole sentence followed by a sentence with a space in the middle.

---

0   I prefer playing tennis to playing squash.

I like playing tennis .... **playing squash.**

- You have to complete the second sentence so that it means the same as the first sentence. You should write one, two or three words in the space.
- You write only the missing words on the answer sheet.

Answer: | **0** | *more than* |

Technique

▼ Read the first sentence and think about what it means. Then read the second sentence, looking at how words are repeated from the first sentence.

▼ Look carefully at the first sentence again and find the phrases and structures which give the sentence its meaning. For example, a comparison, a conditional sentence, quantity, time phrases.

▼ Now look at the second sentence and try to work out which phrase or structure completes it with the same meaning.

▼ Complete the second sentence on the test paper. Don't use more than three words. You may need to use a word from the first sentence.

▼ Read both sentences through again, checking that they mean the same.

Tips

- Practise using the phrases and structures which appear in Writing Part 1, for example, passive to active; different comparisons; conditional sentences and use of *would*; pairs of words like *too* and *enough* and *for* and *since*; reported to direct speech.

TRAINING FOR WRITING PART 1 IN *PET MASTERCLASS*
2.1. MODULE 2 REVIEW. 12.1. MODULE 3 REVIEW. MODULE 4 REVIEW. 19.1. MODULE 5 REVIEW. EXAM TASK 8.2

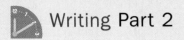

Short message

Facts

- In this Part (Question 6), you write a short note, email, card or postcard.
- The rubric tells you the situation and what type of text to write.

> An English friend of yours called James gave a party yesterday, which you enjoyed.

- The question also gives you three points to include in your answer.

> Write a card to send to James. In your card, you should
> - thank him for the party
> - say what you liked best
> - suggest when you could both meet again.

- You have to write 35–45 words.
- You write your answer on the answer sheet.

Technique

▼ Read the question carefully, making sure you understand the situation, the type of text asked for (note, card, postcard or email) and the points you need to include in your answer.

▼ Start your message with a suitable opening.

▼ Go through each of the three points in the question, writing one or two sentences for each point.

▼ When you have finished, read through your answer. Check that you have included the three points.

▼ Check the length of your answer and shorten it if necessary.

Tips

- Underline the important words in the three points. The verbs they start with tell you a lot about what you have to write, for example, *thank, say, explain, apologise, tell*. Look for other important words, for example, *suggest when* means that you need to give a day, date or time.
- Be careful not to repeat yourself or use words from the question.
- Don't include any extra content in your answer, as this will make it too long.

TRAINING FOR WRITING PART 2 IN *PET MASTERCLASS*
4.2 ALL TEXT TYPES, 6.2 POSTCARD (EXAM TASK), 9.1 EMAIL, 13.1 EMAIL, 17.2 NOTE

Writing Part 3

Letter or story

Facts

- In this Part (Questions 7 or 8) you can choose to write an informal letter **or** a story.
- You should write about 100 words.
- The rubric for the letter includes part of a letter. This tells you what to write in your letter.

> In your next letter, please tell me all about your favourite TV programme. Why do you like watching it? What's it about?

- The rubric for the story gives you the title or the first sentence of the story.

- Your story must have this title:

  ## A surprise visitor

- Your story must begin with this sentence:

  ## I felt nervous when the phone rang.

Technique

▼ Read both questions and decide if you are going to write the letter or the story. Make your decision quickly.

▼ Read the question you chose again and spend a few minutes planning what you are going to write. Make notes on the test paper.

▼ If you write a letter, make sure you include all the information you are asked for. Don't forget to complete the letter by finishing it in a suitable way and signing your name.

▼ If you write a story, make sure that the story you write matches the title, or continues naturally from the sentence you are given. Remember that a story needs to develop from the beginning and have a suitable ending.

▼ Write your letter or story on your answer sheet, thinking carefully about what tenses to use.

▼ Check what you have written. Correct any mistakes.

Tips

- Practise planning and writing short stories. Think about who appears and what happens to them.
- Make sure you know which tenses to use to describe what happens.
- Try to include variety and interest in your writing. Learn different ways to start sentences and use adjectives and adverbs.
- Avoid repeating yourself. Look for this when you check your work and rewrite sentences or cross them out if you have repeated something you have already said.

TRAINING FOR WRITING PART 3 IN *PET MASTERCLASS*

LETTER: 5.2 (EXAM TASK), 10.2, 14.1, 18.2 20.2 STORY: 7.2 (EXAM TASK), 12.2, 16.2, 19.2

Listening Part 1

Short recordings

Facts

- There are seven multiple-choice questions (1–7) with three pictures for each question. There is also an example question.
- The recordings are often about where things are, how something happened, what the time is, or what things someone has.
- For each question you will hear either one or two people speaking. If there are two speakers, they will usually be a man and a woman.
- You hear each recording twice. There are a few seconds before and after each recording.

Technique

▼ Read the question, then look at the pictures and note the differences between them.

▼ Listen carefully to what the speakers say about the things in the pictures.

▼ Put a tick in the box under the picture you think is correct.

▼ You hear the recording again immediately. Check that you have matched the meaning of what you hear with the most suitable picture.

▼ At the end of the test, complete the answer sheet, checking carefully that you are shading the correct lozenges. You are given six minutes to do this.

Tips

- Look at the example question as you listen to the beginning of the recording to familiarise yourself with this Part.
- You may hear words that are in all the pictures so check that you have matched the meaning of what you hear with the most suitable picture.
- Don't panic if you can't decide on the answer the first time. Listen carefully when the recording is repeated.

TRAINING FOR LISTENING PART 1 IN *PET MASTERCLASS*
3.1, 5.2, 9.2, 17.1, EXAM TASK 13.2

Listening Part 2

Detailed meaning

Facts

- There are six multiple-choice questions (8–13) with three possible answers A, B or C.
- There is one main speaker.
- The speaker might talk about their job, life, interests and experiences, or the speaker might be someone like a tour guide, talking to a group of visitors.
- Each question will either be a complete question or the first part of a sentence.
- You are given 45 seconds to read the questions and answers before you hear the recording for the first time.
- You hear the recording twice.

Technique

▼ Use the 45 seconds before you hear the recording to read the questions carefully. Underline the key words.

▼ Read quickly through the possible answers.

▼ During the first listening, put a tick in the box you think is correct.

▼ During the second listening, listen carefully to check that all the information in the answer is correct.

▼ At the end of the test, complete the answer sheet, checking carefully that you are shading the correct lozenges.

Tips

- If you lose your place in the recording, listen out for the key words to the next question(s).
- All the possible answers contain words which you will hear in the recording. Think carefully about which option correctly answers the question or finishes the sentence.

TRAINING FOR LISTENING PART 2 IN *PET MASTERCLASS*
1.2, 6.1, 10.1, 18.1, EXAM TASK 14.2

Listening Part 3

Note completion

Facts

- There are six questions (14–19) which you complete with one or two words or a number.
- There is usually only one speaker.
- The speaker gives information about something, for example, a place, event, course, or person.
- The recording can also be an answerphone message (and may then include three or four different speakers).
- The questions are in the order you hear them in the recording.
- You are given 20 seconds to read the questions before you hear the recording for the first time.
- You hear the recording twice.

Technique

▼ Use the 20 seconds to read quickly through the information given. Underline any key words which will help you to listen for the answer.

▼ Listen out for the key words you've underlined. You may not hear exactly the same words, but you will know to listen for the answer to the question.

▼ Write the missing information quickly in the space. Then keep listening for the next question.

▼ Check your answers when the recording is repeated. If you have to write a long number, for example a phone number, check the order of the numbers you have written carefully.

▼ At the end of the test, write the answers on the answer sheet, checking your spelling carefully.

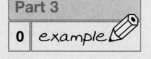

Tips

- The words you need for the answers are exactly as they are in the recording. Don't change them when you write your answer.
- You only need to write one or two words or a number.
- Don't stop to check spelling until the end of the test, when you transfer your answers.

TRAINING FOR LISTENING PART 3 IN *PET MASTERCLASS*
4.2, 8.2, 11.2, 15.1, EXAM TASK 19.2

Listening Part 4

Attitude and opinion

Facts

- There are six sentences (20–25) and you must decide whether they are correct or incorrect.
- You will hear a conversation between two speakers, usually a man and a woman.
- The speakers discuss something. At the end of their conversation there is usually a result.
- The topic of the discussion is given in the rubric.
- You are given 20 seconds to read the sentences before you hear the recording for the first time.
- You hear the recording twice.

Technique

▼ Use the 20 seconds to read quickly through the sentences to see exactly what you will need to listen for.

▼ Listen out for the topic of each sentence. The words you hear are not exactly the same as in the sentence.

▼ Decide whether what you hear means the same as the sentence and put a tick in box A (correct) or B (incorrect).

▼ When you hear the conversation again, listen carefully to check your answers.

▼ At the end of the test, shade the correct lozenges on the answer sheet.

Tips

* Work out from the sentences whether you have to listen for an opinion or a fact.
* Sentences such as *Lucy thinks* or *Lucy is happy to …* are about opinions. You need to decide if the person mentioned (e.g. Lucy) has this opinion.
* Other sentences are statements, for example, *Lucy's friends get more pocket money than she does.* You need to decide if this statement is correct or incorrect.
* Remember: correct = A, incorrect = B.

TRAINING FOR LISTENING PART 4 IN *PET MASTERCLASS*
2.2, 7.2, 16.2, 20.2, EXAM TASK 12.1

The Listening paper lasts for about 30 minutes in total. There are six minutes at the end for you to transfer your answers to the answer sheet.

Speaking Part 1

Facts

* In this first part of the test you are asked simple questions about yourself.
* There will usually be one other candidate, but if you are at the end of a session, you may be in a group of three.
* There are two examiners, but only one will speak (the interlocutor). The other examiner will listen to the candidates.
* The interlocutor will ask each candidate some personal questions, for example about likes and dislikes, daily life.
* At a suitable point, the interlocutor will ask you to spell out something, for example, your name or the country you come from.

Sample Part 1 task

Listen to two PET candidates doing a sample Part 1. Then read these notes about how they perform.

✓ It doesn't matter if you make a mistake in spelling your name, just start again like Gina does. *Listen again and write down Gina's surname.*

✓ Both candidates give detailed answers to the interlocutor's questions, for example Gina's comments about food in Britain and Hana's plans for the weekend. *Listen and make notes about what they say.*

✓ Both candidates use adverbs to make their answers flow and sound more natural, e.g. Gina uses *Actually...* twice and Hana adds to her final answer in Part 1 by agreeing with *exactly.*

Tips

* Try to relax and be confident!
* If you haven't understood, ask the interlocutor to repeat a question.
* Speak clearly, so that both examiners and the other candidate can hear you.
* While the interlocutor is asking the other candidate questions, listen carefully to their voices, to get used to them.
* When answering a question, don't just give one-word answers, give some details.
* Remember the word *because*; this will remind you to give reasons.
* Make sure you can spell in English (revise the letters of the alphabet if necessary, especially letters which are easily confused – *a/e/i;b/v;g/j*, and so on).

TRAINING FOR SPEAKING PART 1 IN *PET MASTERCLASS*
1.1, 2.2, 3.2, 13.2, EXAM TASK 16.1

Speaking Part 2

Facts

- Part 2 tests different language functions, for example making suggestions and agreeing / disagreeing.
- It is a shared task, so you must take turns with your partner and listen to what she / he says.
- You need to work towards a decision, for example, agreeing on a choice.
- To give you some ideas for the task, you will be given a large sheet with pictures on it.
- You will have just a few seconds to think about the task after you get the sheet. The instructions are repeated and then you must start to speak.

Sample Part 2 task

Listen to two PET candidates doing a sample Part 2. Then read these notes about how they perform.

✓ Gina names the friend when she begins, which helps to structure the discussion.

✓ Both candidates are sensitive to turn-taking and invite each other to add to the discussion. *Listen again and write down the phrases they use.*

✓ Patricia's comment on the kinds of music Maria likes is well developed. *Listen again to what she says.*

✗ Some of their answers could be more detailed. *What else could they say about the flowers, the perfume and the pen?*

✗ Notice that both candidates make mistakes, e.g. *a bunch of flower*. However, these errors do not affect the communication between them. Revise plural forms if you need to.

Tips

- Make sure you know what to do. You can ask for the instructions to be repeated again before you start.
- Don't talk all the time. Allow your partner to speak too.
- Use the pictures to help you and say as much as you can about each one before you reach the decision.
- If you don't know a particular word, find a different way to say what you want to. Don't ever say that you don't know something!
- Remember to complete the task and reach a decision with your partner.

TRAINING FOR SPEAKING PART 2 IN *PET MASTERCLASS*
3.2, 5.1, 8.1, 9.2, 14.1, EXAM TASK 11.2

Speaking Part 3

Facts

- Part 3 allows you to speak at greater length on your own about a photograph.
- You need to use a range of vocabulary and show that you can say something about the photograph, even if you don't know all the words in English.
- The two photographs (yours and the one given to the other candidate) are on the same topic.
- You will have a few seconds to think about the task after you get the sheet. Then, the instructions are repeated.

Sample Part 3 task

Listen to two PET candidates doing a sample Part 3. Then read these notes about how they perform.

✗ Candidates are asked here to talk about what they can see in the photograph. Kinga starts to do this, but then moves away from describing the photograph to talk about her holiday experiences. This is not a good idea, as it may mean there is less to say in Part 4. *Listen again to Kinga. What does she say? What else could she say?*

✓ Patricia gives some good description of her photograph, including what someone is wearing, how the people are feeling and what the weather is like. She also suggests where they might be going by coach, using *maybe*. This is a good way to develop this part.

Tips

- Spend a few seconds looking at the photograph carefully and thinking about what you can say.
- Try to talk about everything you can see in the photograph, from the most obvious things to small details, such as what is in the background.
- Don't worry if you don't know a particular word, as the examiners are also looking for your ability to paraphrase and talk around a word you don't know.
- Try to keep talking until the interlocutor tells you to stop.
- Use descriptive phrases rather than just naming the things you can see – for example, don't just say *There's a man* but *There's a rather old man who's wearing strange, old-fashioned clothes…*

TRAINING FOR SPEAKING PART 3 IN *PET MASTERCLASS*
6.2, 7.2, 10.2, 15.1, 17.1, EXAM TASK 18.1

Speaking Part 4

Facts

- Part 4 is a discussion between you and the other candidate (the interlocutor will only speak if the conversation between you stops).
- The discussion will continue the topic of the Part 3 photographs.
- Both candidates should talk for about the same amount of time.

Sample Part 4 task

Listen to two PET candidates doing a sample Part 4. Then read these notes about how they perform.

✗ Patricia starts by asking Kinga 'What would you prefer?' Later in the discussion, this would show good turn-taking skills, but here, it is not fair on the other candidate.

✗ Kinga doesn't answer Patricia's question: she talks about means of transport rather than which type of holiday she prefers. This may be because she has already said what she prefers in Part 3.

✓ There is a bit of discussion during Patricia's answer, with Kinga agreeing at various stages. *Listen to Kinga again. How does she show agreement?*

✓ Patricia also continues Kinga's theme of the campfire effectively. *Listen to her again. What does she talk about?*

✗ In general, the discussion could be developed more. *Look at the pictures again. What other points could they discuss about each type of holiday?*

Tips

- Look at (and talk to) the other candidate, not the interlocutor.
- Try to show an interest in what the other candidate says and invite him or her to comment on your ideas or add to the discussion.
- Don't get angry or unpleasant, even if you don't share the same ideas as the other candidate.
- Don't worry if you disagree, as friendly disagreement can make the discussion more interesting – there is more to say.
- Think of ways to continue the discussion, but don't move away from the topic.

TRAINING FOR SPEAKING PART 4 IN *PET MASTERCLASS*
6.2, 7.2, 12.2, 15.2, 19.1 EXAM TASK 18.2

Vocabulary reference

Unit 1

Daily routines

brush your teeth
eat breakfast / lunch / dinner
get dressed / undressed
get up
go jogging / running / swimming
go to work / college / school
have / take a bath / shower
leave home
lock the door
meet friends
take / catch a bus / train
visit a café / bar

Unit 2

Shopping

advertise	order
buy	pay by cheque
change	pay cash
choose	pay for
complain	price
cost	receipt
customer	return
discount	sell
exchange	take back
goods	

get your money back
pay with a credit card

Clothes

belt	pocket
blouse	pyjamas
boot	shirt
bra	shoe(s)
collar	shorts
dress	skirt
fashion	sleeve
glove	sock(s)
handbag	suit
handkerchief	sweater
hat	T-shirt
jacket	tie
jeans	tights
jumper	trainers
knit (vb)	trousers
(rain) coat	underwear
pants	

Verbs

fit
fold
go with
match
put on
take off
try on
wear out

Unit 3

Parts of the body

ankle	knee
arm	leg
blood	lip
bone	lung
brain	mouth
chest	nail
chin	neck
ear	nose
eye	shoulder
face	skin
finger	stomach
foot / feet	toe
gum	tooth / teeth
hair	throat
hand	thumb
head	tongue
heart	

Illnesses, health problems

(be) sore e.g. *I've got a sore hand.*
break a bone, e.g. *I've broken my arm.*
bruise
cut
cut (yourself) e.g. *I've cut my arm.*
(have) a broken bone, e.g. *I've got a broken arm.*
(have) a cold
(have) a cut e.g. *I've got a cut on my leg.*
(have) a fever
(have) a headache / toothache / stomachache
(have) a pain e.g. *I've got a pain in my leg.*
(have) a sore throat
(have) a temperature
(have) an accident
(have) flu
feel ill

hurt
injure
sprain
wound

Treatments

aspirin
bandage
cure
dressing
(call) an ambulance
get better
(have) an operation
(make) an appointment
medicine
plaster
recover
tablet(s)

Places

dentist's
doctor's
emergency department
hospital
operating theatre

Health

diet
exercise
fit / unfit
healthy / unhealthy

Verbs

balance	sneeze
bend	speak
hitchhike	stand
kiss	taste
point	think
scratch	wave
see	write
smell	

Unit 4

House and home (exterior)

balcony	path
courtyard	roof
garage	shed
garden	terrace
gate	wall
passage	

House and home (interior)

antique	duvet
armchair	fan
bath	hall
bidet	loo
blanket	mirror
blind	painting
bookshelf	pillow
carpet	shower
ceiling	sink
corridor	sofa
cupboard	stairs
curtain	table
cushion	tap
desk	toilet
door	wardrobe
drawers	window

Descriptive adjectives

Size

big	narrow
broad	short
deep	small
large	tiny
long	wide

Shape

oval
round
square (-shaped)

Age

ancient	old
antique	young
modern	20-year-old
new	1980s

Colour

black	pink
blue	purple
brown	red
gold	silver
green	white
grey	yellow
orange	

bright / dark + colour, e.g. *dark blue*
light / pale + colour
blue-grey
blueish-green
yellowish

Nationality

(South) African	Indian
American	Irish
Argentinian	Italian
Australian	Pakistani
Brazilian	Portuguese
British	Russian
Canadian	Scandinavian
European	Scottish
French	Spanish
German	Turkish
Greek	Welsh

Material

cotton	plastic
glass	silk
gold	silver
leather	woollen
metal	

Unit 5

re-

reappear	refill
rearrange	repack
rebuild	repaint
recycle	repay
redevelop	reuse
reenter	rewrite

non-

non-essential
non-fiction
non-slip
non-smoker
non-stop

Places

bay	ocean
beach	port
cliff	rainforest
coast	river
countryside	rock
desert	sand
earth	scenery
east	sea
field	seaside
forest	soil
harbour	south
hedge	stream
hill	valley
lake	waterfall
mountain	west
north	wood

Weather

The letters in brackets show how to make adjectives from the nouns.

climate	rain(y)
cloud(y)	shower
cold	sky
cool	sunshine
damp	thunder
dry	thunderstorm
fine	warm
fog(gy)	wet
freezing	wind(y)
frost(y)	snow
ice (icy)	storm
lightning	sun(ny)
mist(y)	

Unit 6

Sports

athletics	racing
baseball	rugby
basketball	running
boxing	sailing
climbing	skiing
cycling	squash
diving	surfing
fishing	swimming
football	table-tennis
golf	tennis
gymnastics	volleyball
horse-riding	waterskiing
(ice) hockey	windsurfing
motorcycling	

Sports places

court	stadium
pitch	track

Equipment

ball	racket
bat	sail
net	

Actions

hit	race
lose	score
kick	win
play	

Events

competition	match
game	race

People

coach	team
footballer	trainer
player	

Unit 7

Food and drink

bowl	packet
box	plate
buffet	refreshments
candy	roll
cup	seafood
dessert	slice
dish	snack
fork	spoon
fruit juice	spoonful
frying pan	teaspoonful
jar	taste
jug	tin
knife	tube
loaf	vegetarian

Describing taste

bitter	salty
curried	sour
delicious	spicy
fishy	sweet
hot	tasty
rich	

Ways of cooking

bake	grill
boil	microwave
deep-fry	roast
fry	toast

Unit 8

-able

acceptable	photocopiable
affordable	reasonable
comfortable	recyclable
enjoyable	reliable
fashionable	valuable
movable	

-ful

careful	powerful
colourful	thoughtful
doubtful	truthful
helpful	wasteful
hopeful	

Buildings

apartment block /	hotel
block of flats	mosque
castle	office block
cathedral	palace
church	school
cinema	sports centre
cottage	stadium
department store	theatre
factory	tower
gallery	

Materials

brick	plastic
concrete	steel
glass	wood
iron	

Unit 9

Hobbies and interests

collecting things, e.g. *stamps, postcards, CDs, antique furniture*
cooking
dancing
fishing
going out with friends
going to the cinema / theatre / concerts
growing things, e.g. *vegetables, fruit, flowers, plants*
keep fit
listening to music
local history of your town / area
making things, e.g. *sewing clothes painting, drawing, sculpture*
playing a musical instrument
singing
reading
studying a subject, e.g. *a foreign language, history*
taking part in sports
visiting places of interest, e.g. *castles, museums*
walking
watching sports
wildlife

Computers

click	mouse
(go) on-line	screen
keyboard	website
menu	

Unit 10

Music

band	performance
cassette	piano
CD	play
concert	practise
drum	quiet
flute	record
guitar	sing
keyboard	song
loud	stage
musical	synthesizer
musician	trumpet
orchestra	violin
perform	voice

-ed and -ing adjectives

amazed / amazing
amused / amusing
annoyed / annoying
bored / boring
challenged / challenging
disappointed / disappointing
disgusted / disgusting
embarrassed / embarrassing
encouraged / encouraging
entertained / entertaining
excited / exciting
frightened / frightening
interested / interesting
pleased / pleasing
relaxed / relaxing
satisfied / satisfying
surprised / surprising
tired / tiring
worried / worrying

Cinema

audience
film
(main) character
movie
special effects

Unit 11

Travel and holidays

What to do before a holiday

apply for a visa
arrange holiday insurance
book flights
change money
find a hotel / camp-site / holiday cottage
make a reservation
pay a deposit

What to take on holiday

backpack
camera
currency
driving licence
first aid kit
guidebook
insect repellent
map
passport
swimming costume
suitcase
sun cream / lotion
sunglasses
sun hat

Unit 12

Personal relationships

best friend   husband
boyfriend   partner
classmate   wife
girlfriend

get... divorced / engaged / married

Relationships at work

boss   employee
colleague   employer

Family relationships

aunt   grandmother
brother   mother
cousin   nephew
daughter   niece
father   sister
grandchild   son
grandfather   uncle

Phrasal verbs

go out with   split up
hold on   walk out on

Unit 13

Means of transport

ambulance   hovercraft
bicycle / bike   hydrofoil
boat   jet
bus   motorbike
cab   scooter
camel   ship
car   taxi
coach   train
ferry   tram
helicopter   underground
horse

Prepositional phrases

at first   least
    home   that moment
    last   work
by accident   post
    bus   sight
    hand   train
    mistake   yourself
    plane
in advance   half
    a hurry   love
    any case   order to
    case of (fire) time
    danger   turn
    fact
on board   request
    foot   sale
    holiday   time
    purpose

Unit 14

Means of communication

card   letter
email   (mobile) phone
fax   postcard

Using email

forward (vb)
reply (vb)
send (vb)

Language and customs

ancient   original
chat   publish
dialect   shout (vb)
dictionary   signal (vb)
festival   speech
grammar   text (vb)
local   traditional
message   translation

Unit 15

Services

book   tickets to the theatre
make   an appointment
                   a reservation
                   a complaint
order   a CD
pay   your mobile phone
                     bill
reserve   a room in a hotel
                   a table in a restaurant
have / get   a pizza delivered
                   your bike repaired

your car washed
your clothes cleaned
your eyes tested
your hair cut
your laundry ironed
some flowers
   delivered
new clothes made
your rubbish/recycling
   collected
your house repaired/
   painted/decorated
your gardening done

Places where you are offered services

bank   hairdresser's
café   hotel
dentist's   photocopy shop
doctor's   photographer's
dressmaker's   post-office
drycleaner's   restaurant
florist's

Unit 16

Emotions, feelings, experiences

Adjectives

afraid   fond of
amused   guilty
angry   happy
anxious   miserable
ashamed   nervous
awful   pleasant
bored   sad
delighted   satisfied
depressed   surprised
embarrassed   worried
excited

Verbs

apologise   dream
argue   embarrass
behave   excuse
believe   feel
blame   forgive
care about   frighten
cheat   insist
discuss   persuade

have an argument
make someone nervous, happy, etc.

un-

unafraid	unhealthy
unashamed	uninterested
unattractive	unkind
unclear	unknown
unembarassed	unlucky
unemployed	unnatural
unexcited	unnecessary
unexpected	unpleasant
unfair	untidy
unfashionable	unusual
unfriendly	unwell
unhappy	

-less

blameless	heartless
careless	helpless
childless	homeless
endless	hopeless
faultless	priceless
fearless	thoughtless
harmless	useless

Unit 17

Jobs

actor / actress	lawyer
architect	lecturer
artist	librarian
banker	lifeguard
chef	mechanic
chemist	model
cook	novelist
customs officer	nurse
dancer	operator
dentist	photographer
designer	pilot
detective	police officer
disc jockey	porter
doctor	postman
engineer	priest
farmer	programmer
fire fighter	reporter
grocer	sailor
guard	salesman /
hairdresser	woman
instructor	scientist
journalist	secretary
judge	shop assistant
labourer	travel agent

General job titles

assistant
boss
businessman / woman
colleague
director
manager
president
staff

Other

career	employment
certificate	fee
conference	full-time
contract	part-time
degree	pay
diploma	profession
employ	professional
(self-)employed	qualification
(un-)employed	retire
employee	salary
employer	wages

Unit 18

Compound adjectives

big-headed	low-paid
broken-down	made-up
broken-hearted	never-ending
cut-price	nice-looking
full-grown	old-fashioned
full-length	one-sided
good-looking	one-way
half-price	right-handed
home-made	short-sighted
ice-cold	trouble-free
last-minute	well-behaved
left-handed	well-dressed
life-size	well-known
long-distance	world-famous
long-lasting	year-long
long-lost	

Unit 19

Animals

Farm animals

bull	horse
chicken	lamb
cow	pig
goat	sheep

Pets

cat	kitten
dog	puppy
hamster	rabbit

Wild animals

bear	monkey
camel	shark
dolphin	snake
elephant	tiger
giraffe	whale
lion	zebra

Unit 20

Subjects

art
biology
chemistry
computer studies / computing
economics
education
geography
history
information technology (IT)
languages
mathematics / maths
music
physics
science
technology

Exams

exam paper
fail
mark
pass
results

-ment

agreement	enjoyment
announcement	entertainment
arrangement	involvement
development	judgement
disappointment	management
disagreement	payment
employment	punishment
encouragement	

-ation

communication	organisation
consideration	preparation
education	qualification
examination	registration
explanation	reservation
imagination	

Grammar reference

Unit 1

Some / any

We use *some* in affirmative sentences to talk about

- a quantity (with uncountable nouns).
  I'd like some information.
  We've got some luggage to check in.

- a number (with countable nouns).
  Harry bought some new books yesterday.
  There are some bananas in the fruit bowl.

Note: *bit* and *piece* are often used with uncountable nouns to make the phrase countable.
  two good bits of advice, several pieces of luggage

In negative sentences, we use *any*.
  There wasn't any information.
  There wasn't ~~some~~ information.

In questions, we usually use *any*.
  Do you need any money?

However in questions where the answer is likely to be 'yes', *some* is used. It is also used

- in offers.
  Would you like some coffee?

- in requests.
  Could you give me some advice?

Any is also used in general affirmative statements.
  Any type of exercise will make you feel better.

Past simple

Regular verbs

Affirmative	Negative	Interrogative
subj + verb + *-ed*	subj + *didn't* + verb	*did(n't)* + subj + verb + ?

Irregular verb table

Base form	Past simple	Past participle
be	was / were	been
become	became	become
begin	began	begun
break	broke	broken
bring	brought	brought
build	built	built
buy	bought	bought
can	could	could
choose	chose	chosen
come	came	come
cost	cost	cost
cut	cut	cut
do	did	done
dream	dreamed	dreamed
drink	drank	drunk
drive	drove	driven
eat	ate	eaten
fall	fell	fallen
feed	fed	fed
feel	felt	felt
fight	fought	fought
find	found	found
fly	flew	flown
forget	forgot	forgotten
get	got	got
give	gave	given
go	went	gone
have	had	had
hear	heard	heard
hide	hid	hidden
hit	hit	hit
hold	held	held
hurt	hurt	hurt
keep	kept	kept
know	knew	known
learn	learned	learned
leave	left	left
lend	lent	lent
let	let	let
lie	lay	lain
lose	lost	lost
make	made	made
mean	meant	meant
meet	met	met
pay	paid	paid
put	put	put
read	read	read
ride	rode	ridden
ring	rang	rung
run	ran	run

Base form	Past simple	Past participle
say	said	said
see	saw	seen
sell	sold	sold
send	sent	sent
set	set	set
shake	shook	shaken
shine	shone	shone
show	showed	shown / showed
shut	shut	shut
sing	sang	sung
sit	sat	sat
sleep	slept	slept
speak	spoke	spoken
spend	spent	spent
split	split	split
spread	spread	spread
stand	stood	stood
steal	stole	stolen
swim	swam	swum
take	took	taken
teach	taught	taught
tell	told	told
think	thought	thought
try	tried	tried
understand	understood	understood
wear	wore	worn
win	won	won
write	wrote	written

We use the past simple to talk about

- things that happened in the past.
  I went shopping at the weekend.

- past states.
  He was a very happy child.

- past habits.
  I walked to school every day in the summer.

Past continuous

Affirmative	Negative	Interrogative
subj + *was* / *were* + verb + *-ing*	subj + *wasn't* / *weren't* + verb + *-ing*	*was(n't)* / *were(n't)* + subj + verb + *-ing* + ?

We use the past continuous to talk about

- temporary situations in the past.
  I was feeling ill yesterday.

- activities in progress at a particular time in the past.
  At eight o'clock last night, I was watching TV.

- a situation in the past that is interrupted by an action or event. The verb connected with this action or event is in the past simple tense.

SEE UNIT 6 FOR VERBS WHICH ARE NOT USED IN CONTINUOUS FORMS.

Unit 2

Comparisons

Adjectives

Adjective		Comparative	Superlative
Single syllable	*cheap*	*cheaper*	*the cheapest*
Two syllables ending in *-y*	*pretty*	*prettier*	*the prettiest*
Two syllable ending in *-ful*, or *-ly*	*careful*	*more / less careful*	*the most / least careful*
Three or more syllables	*powerful*	*more / less powerful*	*the most / least powerful*

Irregular comparisons

good	better	the best
bad	worse	the worst
little	less	the least
many	more	the most
much	more	the most

> CDs are <u>more expensive</u> in this shop <u>than</u> at Our Price.
> Plastic shoes <u>are cheaper than</u> leather ones.
> The food here is <u>as expensive as</u> the food in restaurants in London.
> Leather shoes are <u>not as cheap as</u> plastic ones.
> The CDs in Our Price are <u>less expensive than</u> in this shop.
> These are <u>the most expensive</u> sunglasses in the shop.
> Ray Ban sunglasses are the most stylish of all sunglasses.

Adverbs

Adverb		Comparative	Superlative
Single syllable (and *early*)	*fast*	*faster*	*fastest*
Two or more syllables	*carefully*	*more carefully*	*most carefully*

Irregular comparisons

well	better	best
badly	worse	worst
little	less	least
much	more	most

> I drive as fast as my brother.
> People drive more quickly than they did 30 years ago.
> Young people drive less carefully than other people.
> Sasha speaks French the most fluently in our class.
> Oasis played the loudest of all the bands at the concert.

SEE UNIT 6 FOR POSITION OF ADVERBS OF FREQUENCY.

Unit 3

Ability

	Affirmative	Negative
Present	*can / am able*	*can't / am not able*
Past	simple past: *could / was able* present perfect: *have been able* past perfect: *had been able*	*could not /* *was not able* present perfect: *have not been able* past perfect: *had not been able*
Future	*will be able*	*will not/won't be able*

Possibility

	Affirmative	Negative
Present	*may / might / could*	*may not* (~~mayn't~~) *might not / mightn't,* *could not / couldn't*
Past	*may / might /* *could have* + past participle	*may not* (~~mayn't~~) *might not /mightn't,* *have* + past participle
Future	*may / might /could*	*may not* (~~mayn't~~) *might not / mightn't,* *could not / couldn't*

Note: for the PET exam you do not need to talk about possibility in the past.

There is no *s* for the *he / she / it* verb form.
> *I might have a temperature.*
> *She might have a temperature.*

After *can, may, might* and *could* we use an infinitive without *to*. After *be able to* we use an infinitive with *to*.

We do not use an auxiliary verb with *may, might* and *could*.

We can use *may* and *might* with question words.
> *When might he arrive?*

To make questions without a question word, we use
> *Do you think.*

> *Do you think he's got a temperature?*
> *Do you think you will need an operation?*

Can't / Couldn't means 'there is no possibility'.
> *My leg can't be broken* means that my leg is definitely not broken.

We use *can* in the passive.
> *Emergency appointments can be made between 5p.m. and 6p.m. every evening.*

- We use *could* or *be able* to talk about past ability.
  I could walk properly again two weeks after the accident.
- If we want to talk about ability and an action in the past we use *was able*.
  Although I was hurt quite badly in the accident, I was able to get out of the car and call for help.

Unit 4

Imperatives

Affirmative imperatives have the same form as the base form. Negative imperatives are formed with *do not/don't* + infinitive.
> *Start your message now.*
> *Don't leave luggage unattended*

We use the imperative to
- give advice.
- give directions.
  'Go down this street, take the first turning on the right and the sports stadium is at the bottom of the hill.'
- give instructions.
  To make hot chocolate, put a mug of milk into a saucepan. Add the chocolate powder …
- give warnings.
- make suggestions.
- tell people what to do.

Unit 5

The passive

Active   The Remarkable Company *makes* pencils from plastic cups.
Passive Pencils *are made* from plastic cups.

The object of the active sentence (pencils) becomes the subject of the passive sentence.

The verb *be* in the passive sentence is in the same form as the active sentence.

Tense	Passive	Example sentence
Present simple	*am/are/is* + past participle	Mouse mats are made from old tyres.
Present continuous	*am/are/is being* + past participle	Readers are being asked to join the recycling scheme.
Past simple	*was/were* + past participle	Millions of bottles were thrown away last year.
Past continuous	*was/were being* + past participle	All along the beach birds were being covered in spilt oil.
Present perfect	*have/has been* + past participle	Recycled products have been developed.
Future with *will*	*will be* + past participle	More rubbish will be recycled in the future.
Future with *going to*	*am/are/is going to be* + past participle	I wonder if other schools are going to be involved in the recycling programme.

We use the passive to say what happens, or what is done to something/body when the focus is mainly on the action, event or process, not on who does it.

> *A lot of jewellery was stolen from her room* (passive).
> *Somebody stole a lot of jewellery from her room* (active).

We use the passive when
- it's not important who does the action.
- we don't know who does the action.
- people in general do the action.

When we want to say who does the action we use *by*.
> *Recycled pencils are made <u>by</u> The Remarkable Company.*
> *Old mobile phones are being collected <u>by</u> students at Swinford High School.*

We can use modal verbs with passives, using *be* in the infinitive.
> *Old printer cartridges <u>can be cleaned</u> and refilled.*
> *In some countries rubbish <u>must be sorted</u> into different bins.*

Unit 6

Adverbs of frequency

We put adverbs of frequency
- after *be* and auxiliary verbs
  I am always late for my yoga class.
  I have never been climbing.
- before other verbs
  Ray rarely does any exercise.
  Jane usually has a run in the morning before work.

Usually, often, sometimes can go at the beginning or the end of a sentence.
> *Sometimes we go horse-riding at the weekend.*
> *Dave plays squash sometimes.*

We form questions like this:
> *How often do you ...?*
> *Have you ever been climbing?*
> *Do you always swim after work?*

SEE UNIT 2 FOR COMPARISON OF ADVERBS.

Present simple

Affirmative	Negative	Interrogative
subj + verb (+ -s/ -es)	subj + *don't/ doesn't* + verb	*do/does* + subj + verb + ?

Note: most verbs add *-s* to *he/she/it* forms, but some verbs need other changes.
hurry, carry   *hurries, carries*
watch, push, miss   *watches, pushes, misses*

We use the simple present
- to talk about definite facts and permanent situations.
  There are eleven players in a football team.
  Football is the national sport in Brazil.
- to talk about regular events and activities.
  The Olympic Games take place every four years.
  Jim trains at the gym every Monday and Thursday.

Present continuous

Affirmative	Negative	Interrogative
subj + *am/are/ is* + verb + *-ing*	subj + *am/are/ is + not* + verb + *-ing*	*am/are/is* + subj + verb + *-ing* + ?

We use the present continuous
- to talk about actions and situations which are happening now or for a short time.
  The radio presenter is interviewing Dave about his sports experience.
- to talk about temporary actions and situations which may happen for a longer period, but are not permanent.
  Dave's training for the World Championships next year.

We don't normally use these verbs in the present continuous.

- verbs connected to the senses
  feel, hear, see, smell, appear, look (meaning *seem*), *sound, taste*
- verbs connected to emotions and thinking
  believe, dislike, doubt, feel (meaning *have an opinion*), *imagine, know, like, love, hate, prefer, realise, recognise, remember, see* (meaning *understand*), *think* (meaning *have an opinion*), *understand, want, wish*
- other verbs
  be, agree, disagree, impress, satisfy, promise, surprise

Unit 7

Zero conditional

If / *When* + subj + present tense, subj + present tense

> *If I eat too much chocolate, I get a headache.*
> *When milk goes off, it tastes sour.*

We use the zero conditional to talk about things that are true.

First conditional

If / *Unless* + subj + present tense, subj + *will (won't)* + infinitive

> *If I visit Italy, I'll buy you some sun-dried tomatoes.*
> *Unless you take the cake out of the oven now, it'll burn.*

Subj + *will (won't)* + infinitive *if/unless* + subj + present tense

> *Helen will join us at the restaurant if she has time.*
> *They won't give you a vegetarian meal unless you order one in advance.*

We use the first conditional to talk about possible or likely events in the future, given a certain condition.

Using *unless*

The word *unless* means 'if not', so you cannot follow it with a negative verb. On the other hand, *if* can be followed by a negative verb.

> *You won't be able to cook this dish unless you have real Indian spices.*
> *You won't be able to cook this dish if you don't have real Indian spices.*

SEE UNIT 16 FOR THE SECOND CONDITIONAL.

Unit 8

Present perfect

Affirmative	Negative	Interrogative
subj + *has* / *have* + past participle	subj + *hasn't* / *haven't* + past participle	*has(n't)* / *have(n't)* + subj + past participle + ?

We use the present perfect to talk about

- a recent event or action.
  I've bought a ticket for Michael Moore's show.
  Zola has just scored a second goal for Chelsea.
- something which started in the past and is still continuing.
  The cinema has been open since 1998.
  Jack has lived in the flat upstairs for ages.
- something that happened in the past but we don't know when.
  Melbourne has hosted the Olympic Games.

However, we use the past simple to talk about something that happened at a particular time in the past.

> *Sydney hosted the Olympic Games in 2000.*

Note: *Ever* and *never* have a different meaning. *Ever* means at any point in your life, *never* means at no point in your life.

> *Have you ever been inside a palace?*
> *I've never climbed to the top of that tower.*

Relative pronouns

In relative clauses we use

- *who* to talk about people.
  Sarah, who is an architect, is going to draw up some plans for us.
- *which* or *that* to talk about things.
  The school, which is nearly 100 years old, will be pulled down next month.
  The cinema that we went to is quite near the city centre.
- *where* to talk about places.
  The cottage where we stayed last summer is for sale.

- *whose* to talk about things that belong to people or places.
  The elderly couple, whose house was damaged in the high winds, are staying with friends.
  The new building, whose unusual shape is a bit like a huge gherkin, can be seen from the river.

You cannot use *what*.
  The castle ~~what~~ I visited was very interesting.
Instead, you must use *which* or *that*.

Unit 9

Verbs followed by *-ing*

We add *-ing* to verbs to make an '-ing form'. This often acts like a noun, e.g. *swimming, playing*. We use this form after these verbs.

admit avoid consider delay detest dislike enjoy feel like finish forgive give up (can't) help imagine involve keep on mention mind miss practise put off risk (can't) stand suggest understand

  I enjoy looking for bargains on the internet.
  I enjoy ~~to look for~~ …
  Leo suggested having a website for the tennis club.
  Leo suggested ~~to have~~ …
  The doctor has told me I must give up eating cheese.
  The doctor has told me I must give up ~~to eat~~ …

Prepositions followed by *-ing*

If we use a verb immediately after a preposition, we use the *-ing* form of the verb.
  After looking at lots of different websites, I finally found the information I wanted.
  You can't use the web without dialling up a connection.
  Close all programs before switching off the computer.

Note: *To* can be part of an infinitive, e.g. *to shop, to write*, or it can be a preposition. When it is a preposition, we can follow it with a noun or a verb. If we want to use a verb we need to use the *-ing* form.

I look forward to your next email.
Here *to* is a preposition followed by a noun phrase.

I look forward to seeing you next week.
Here *to* is a preposition followed by a verb in the *-ing* form.

Unit 10

Obligation

We use *must* to talk about a strong obligation.
  You must bring a towel with you.
  Visitors to the festival must buy tickets in advance.

Using *must* also tells us that the speaker is putting the obligation on themselves.
  I must give up smoking.

must

There is no *-s* for the *he / she / it* verb form.
  He must work eight hours each day he's at the festival.

After *must* we use an infinitive without *to*.

We do not use an auxiliary verb with *must* for negatives or questions.
  Visitors must not smoke in their tents.
  You mustn't play loud music at the camping site.
  Must I wear a uniform to work here?

have to

We can also use *have (got) to* to talk about a strong obligation, often when we talk about what someone else expects of us. We can also use *need* here.
  I have to take a towel when I stay in the festival accommodation.
  The doctor says I have to give up smoking.
  I need to buy my ticket before I go to the festival.

We use *have to*, not *must* when we talk about obligation in the past and future.
  We had to order our tickets on the internet a month before the festival.
  I will have to work hard if I want to be a steward at Glastonbury this year.

Prohibition

We use *must not / mustn't* to talk about what we are not allowed to do. We cannot use *not have to* to talk about a negative obligation or prohibition.
  Visitors mustn't arrive at the festival site before 12p.m.
  ~~Visitors don't have to arrive at the festival site before 12 p.m.~~

Lack of obligation

We use *don't have to* or *needn't* to talk about situations where there is no obligation to do something.
  We don't need to take our tent.
  I don't have to buy my ticket in advance.

Don't have to means *don't need to*. It does not mean the same as *mustn't*.

Unit 11

Past simple and past perfect

Affirmative	Negative	Interrogative
subj + *had* + past participle	subj + *hadn't* + past participle	*had(n't)* + subj + past participle + ?

We use the past perfect tense to make it clear that one event or action happened earlier than another. The past simple tense is used for the later event or action.

> *I had stayed in Lisbon in 1997, so I knew my way around the city quite well.*
> *Mark hadn't had much time to pack and arrived at the hotel without any toothpaste.*

> *Before you took the job in Rome, had you worked anywhere else in Italy?*

When it is not necessary to make the time difference clear, the past simple tense can be used (see unit 1 for information on its formation).

> *I worked in Bolivia and Argentina before I moved to Spain, so my Spanish was quite good.*

SEE UNIT 1 FOR A LIST OF IRREGULAR VERB PARTICIPLES.

Unit 12

Reported speech

The actual words that someone uses are called **direct speech**. When these words are reported by someone else, **reported speech** is used. When this happens there is usually a tense change backwards in time.

Present simple > past simple
Marta said: 'I don't remember him.'
Marta said she didn't remember him.

Present continuous > past continuous
Jack said: 'I'm looking for my sister.'
Jack said he was looking for his sister.

Past simple > past perfect
Robert said: 'Michael emailed me about a new project.'
Robert said Michael had emailed him about a new project.

Present perfect > past perfect
Ellen said: 'I've met an Australian artist.'
Ellen said she had met an Australian artist.

will > would
'I will finish work later than usual today.'
Clare said she would finish work later than usual today.

can > could
Wendy asked me 'Can you play the guitar?'
Wendy asked me if I could play the guitar.

say / speak / talk / tell

These verbs are commonly confused.

We use *say*

- with someone's actual words.
  I said: 'How are you?'
- in reported speech.
  Yannis said that he could come for a meal on Friday.

We use *talk* not *say*

- about something that a person is discussing.
  Sally talked about her new house.
  ~~Sally said about her new house.~~

We use *tell*

- when both the speaker and the listener are mentioned.
  Patrick has told his brother to move out of the flat.

We cannot use *tell*

- without an object.
  Chris told a funny story to the children.
  ~~Chris told to the children.~~

We use *speak*

- with or without an object.
  Chris spoke to the children.
  I speak a little Polish.
  Speak up, we can't hear you!
  Ken spoke for a few minutes at the beginning of the meeting.

Note: When a question is reported we don't need to add a question mark.

Unit 13

Will / shall

Affirmative	Negative	Interrogative
subj + *will* / *shall* + infinitive without *to*	subj + *won't* / *shan't* + infinitive without *to*	*shall* / *will* + subj + infinitive without *to* + ?

We use *will*

- to make an offer.
  I'll lend you my car, if you like.
- to make a promise.
  We'll keep in touch by email while we're away.
- to make a prediction (say what you think will happen) about the future.
  Increased air travel will also damage the environment.

Shall is mainly used for questions in the first person.
> *Shall I pick you up around seven tomorrow night?*

Unit 14

Used to

We use *used to* to talk about things that happened in the past but don't now.

> *There used to be many more dialects in Britain than there are now.*
> *I used to be able to speak fluent Spanish as a child, but I've forgotten most of it now.*

When asking questions using *used to*, it is often possible to use two different forms, though the examples in brackets are less common.

> *Did you use to (used to) speak in dialect with your grandmother?*
> *How did you use to (used to) get to school?*

If you are asking a question without *did*, you can only use *used to*.

> *Which people used to speak Ladino?*

Tag questions

These are quite common in spoken English and are mainly used when the speaker expects someone to agree or confirm something. The 'tag' is always added at the end of the sentence and repeats the main verb, in a negative or affirmative form.

A negative tag is used with an affirmative sentence.

> *The Valencian flag is blue, red and yellow, isn't it?*
> *Dialects are still quite widely used in Italy, aren't they?*
> *There's a lot of interest in the Basque language, isn't there?*

An affirmative tag is used with a negative sentence.

> *You aren't the only Corsican living here, are you?*
> *Catalan didn't use to be taught in schools, did it?*
> *The students won't understand the Sicilian dialect used in the film, will they?*

If the main verb in the sentence is an affirmative form of *be* or an auxiliary verb, you form the tag like this:

Main verb	Tag
am	aren't I?
are	aren't you/we/they?
is	isn't he/she/it?
have	haven't I/you/we/they?
has	hasn't he/she/it?
do	don't I/you/we/they?
does	doesn't he/she/it?
did	didn't I/you/he/she/it/we/they?
will	won't I/you/he/she/it/we/they?
should	shouldn't I/you/he/she/it/we/they?
must	mustn't I/you/he/she/it/we/they?
can	can't I/you/he/she/it/we/they?
could	couldn't I/you/he/she/it/we/they?

If the main verb in the sentence is not *be* or an auxiliary, you use *don't, doesn't* or *didn't*.

> *You speak to your grandmother in Provençal, don't you?*
> *They publish a Basque dictionary, don't they?*

Unit 15

Have / get something done

Affirmative	Negative	Interrogative
subj + *have / get* + obj + past participle (+ extra information)	subj + *don't / doesn't + have / get* + object (+ extra information)	*do / does* + subj + *have / get* + obj (+ extra information) + ?

I have my hair cut every six weeks.

They don't have their flat cleaned.
Where do you get your dry cleaning done?

Get something done is more informal than *have* something done.

Future forms: *will, going to,* present continuous

Predictions

We use *will* to make predictions and give information about the future

- when we don't talk about a particular time in the future.
  I'll be home before you.

- when the speaker is saying what he / she thinks, believes, hopes, etc. will happen.
  It will be so nice to see Marie again.
  I wonder what the weather will be like in Canada.
  Dina and her mother will be at the party.

We use *going to* to make predictions about the future

- when we have evidence to suggest something is going to happen.
  She's going to have a baby.

- when we are talking about the near future.
  It's going to snow – look at the clouds.
  The car's making a terrible noise. It's going to break down soon.

Sometimes both *will* and *going to* are possible, but we never use *will* to make predictions based on evidence.

Intentions, plans and arrangements

We use *will* to talk about intentions which we haven't thought about before we speak.

A   *My car's at the garage.*
B   *I'll give you a lift to work.*

A   *Ruth's not very well.*
B   *I'll send her a card.*

We use *going to* to talk about intentions and plans we've thought about before we speak.

> *I've bought some eggs. I'm going to make Lucy a birthday cake.*
> *Dave's got a new job in Scotland, so he's going to sell his flat and move.*

A   *What do you need the map for?*
B   *I'm going to work out a route to Gary's house.*

We can use either *will* or *going to* to talk about an intention we have neither clearly thought about beforehand, nor just decided on.

> *One day we're going to / we will travel round the world.*
> *I'm going to / I'll tell you a secret.*

We use the present continuous for definite arrangements in the future. *Going to* is also possible, but the present continuous is more likely if arrangements are already fixed and organised.

> *I'm seeing Jeff on Thursday evening.*
> *Polly's getting her hair cut after college today.*

Unit 16

Second conditional

If + simple past, *would* + infinitive

> *If my brother was in trouble, I would do everything to help him.*

would + infinitive + *if* + simple past

> *I might have a big wedding if I found someone I really loved.*
> *Val could go out in the evenings if she finished her homework earlier.*

We sometimes use *were* instead of *was* after *I*, especially when giving advice.

If I were you, I would …

We use the second conditional

- to talk about situations which do not exist.
  I would go to college on the bus if I didn't have so many books to carry. (But I have a lot of books to carry therefore I go in the car.)

- to talk about unlikely future situations.
  If I won the lottery, I would stop working. (But I'm unlikely to win the lottery, so it's unlikely I'll stop working.)

We can use *could* or *might* in the main clause to introduce a meaning of ability or possibility.

> *If I had enough money, I could rent a bigger flat.*
(I don't have enough money, therefore I am unable to move to a bigger flat.)

> *If Kerry's friend needed his help, he might lie for him.*
(It is possible that Kerry would lie for his friend, but not definite.)

Unit 17

Infinitives

After many verbs we can use another verb in the infinitive with *to*. Here are some verbs like this:

afford	*choose*	*manage*
agree	*continue*	*offer*
appear	*decide*	*need*
arrange	*fail*	*warn*
begin	*learn*	

By Tuesday afternoon I had <u>begun to understand</u> my new job.
Ken <u>chose not to tell</u> his boss about the missing papers.
I'm <u>waiting to find</u> out if I've got the job.

- We use an object + infinitive (with *to*) after these verbs. We cannot use *that* after these verbs.

allow	*leave*	*request*
ask	*order*	*teach*
expect	*persuade*	*tell*
encourage	*prefer*	*want*
hope	*recommend*	
invite	*remind*	

My boyfriend <u>encouraged me to apply</u> for the job.
My boyfriend encouraged ~~that I~~ …
The management <u>wants the staff to take</u> shorter breaks.
The management ~~wants that the staff~~ …

- We can also use an infinitive (with *to*) after a noun or a word like *anywhere, someone*, etc.
  Kate asked someone to help her with the post.
  I haven't got the information to finish the report.

- Some verbs which are followed by an infinitive with *to* show a thinking action, e.g. *agree, hope, expect.*
  I'm expecting to hear the sales results this afternoon.
  I agreed not to talk about the new plans for the company.

- We can talk about the purpose of an action using a verb followed by an infinitive with *to*. We can also use the phrase *in order (not) to*, to talk about purpose.
  A customer <u>rang to complain</u> about our products.
  Tina bought a mobile phone <u>in order not to</u> miss calls from her boss.

Unit 18

Quantity

Uncountable nouns	Uncountable and countable nouns	Countable nouns
a little / a bit (of)	no / not... any / none some a lot of / lots of / plenty of	a few several, a number of

A bit of success is all you need to get you noticed.

Did you win any prizes as a child?
Don't feel sorry for film stars – they've got plenty of money.
There are a number of different competitions in the film and TV industry.

	some	any	no	every
-one	someone	anyone	no one	everyone
-body	somebody	anybody	nobody	everybody
-thing	something	anything	nothing	everything
-where	somewhere	anywhere	nowhere	everywhere

You can always find somewhere to park in town after the shops close.
It was late, I had lost my keys to the flat and I had nowhere to go.
Everybody was staring at me – what did they think I'd done?

Note: *-one* and *-body* mean the same.

Unit 19

So / neither / nor

You say	Your partner agrees with you
I agree.	So do I.
I don't agree.	Neither / Nor do I.
I'm sure	So am I.
I'm not sure.	Nor / Neither am I.

I'm going out this evening. So am I.
I'm not going out this evening. Neither / Nor am I.

I passed my exam. Neither / Nor did I.
I was watching TV. So was I.
I wasn't watching TV. Neither / Nor was I.
I've had lunch. So have I.
I haven't had lunch. Neither / Nor have I.

Using *so*, *neither* or *nor* shows that your own opinion or action is (or was) the same as someone else's.
Anna likes penguins and <u>so do I</u>.
Anna bought a book on penguins and <u>so did I</u>.

Neither and *nor* are both used to agree with a negative statement.
Anna didn't want to go home and neither did I.

Any two people, places or things can be compared in this way.
Harry has worked at Melbourne Zoo and so has Chris.
London has a zoo and so does Bristol.
The zoo shop wasn't open and nor was the café.
Snakes don't frighten Ray and neither do spiders.

Unit 20

Possesive forms

Most genitives are formed by adding an apostrophe with or without *-s*.
my sister's application (the application my sister has prepared)
Jonathan's work placement (the work placement that Jonathan is doing)
the children's homework (the homework of the children)

The possessive pronouns *mine, yours, his, hers, ours, theirs* are sometimes used in phrases with *of*.
a friend of his
a book of theirs

We can emphasise the genitive relationship by using *own*.
Nature's own recipe
Ellen's own money

OXFORD
UNIVERSITY PRESS

Great Clarendon Street, Oxford OX2 6DP

Oxford University Press is a department of the University of Oxford.
It furthers the University's objective of excellence in research,
scholarship, and education by publishing worldwide in

Oxford New York

Auckland Bangkok Buenos Aires Cape Town Chennai
Dar es Salaam Delhi Hong Kong Istanbul Karachi Kolkata
Kuala Lumpur Madrid Melbourne Mexico City Mumbai Nairobi
São Paulo Shanghai Taipei Tokyo Toronto

Oxford and Oxford English are registered trade marks of
Oxford University Press in the UK and in certain other countries

© Oxford University Press 2003

The moral rights of the author have been asserted

Database right Oxford University Press (maker)

First published 2003

ISBN 0 19 4514005

Printed and bound by Grafiasa S.A. in Portugal

ACKNOWLEDGEMENTS
The authors and publisher are grateful to those who have given
permission to reproduce the following extracts and adaptations of
copyright material:
pp8-9 'Why you should trust your instincts' by Fiona McDonald, *She*
November 2002 © National Magazine Company. Reproduced by
permission.
p21 'A house and it's horses' by Patricia Morrison © *House and Garden*
/ The Condé Nast Publications Ltd. Reproduced by permission.
p28 Information about Remarkable Environmental Products from
www.remarkable.co.uk. Reproduced by permission.
p28 'Local school plans turn trash into cash' from Eurosource Europe
Limited www.esel.co.uk. Reproduced by permission.
p33 'Going the distance' © Andy Darling, *Observer* 27 October 2002.
Reproduced by permission of Guardian Newspapers Limited.
p36 'Meals on wheels' © Sheila Keating / Times Newspapers Limited
12 September 1998. Reproduced by permission.
p53 Information from www.glastonburyfestivals.co.uk. Reproduced by
permission.
p56 Case study from Raleigh International expedition guide.
Reproduced by permission of Raleigh International.
p68 'Coming of age – the travel of young adults' by Sally Cairns,
Town and Country Planning April 2000. Reproduced by permission
of Sally Cairns.
p74 Extract from Mother Tongues by Helen Drysdale © Helen
Drysdale 2001. Reproduced by permission of Macmillan
Publishers Ltd.

p90-91 'Vacation deficit disorder' by Marsha Scarborough from
www.futurestep.com. Reproduced by permission of Korn/Ferry
International.
p96 Information about Project Tiger from www.cathouse-fcc.org.
Reproduced by permission.
p98 Information about Undersea Explorer Expeditions from
www.undersea.com.au. Reproduced by permission.
p6 reproduced by permission of the University of Cambridge Local
Examinations Syndicate

Although every effort has been made to trace and contact copyright
holders before publication, this has not been possible in some cases.
We apologise for any apparent infringement of copyright and if
notified, the publisher will be pleased to rectify any errors or
omissions at the earliest opportunity.

Sources:
p72 New Scientist April 2002
p92 abcnews.com, Total Film April 2002, J17 April 2002

We would like to thank the following for permission to reproduce photographs:
Alamy pp13b (National Motor Museum/Motoring Picture Library),
27c (Colin Walton), 27tl (David Hoffman/David Hoffman Photo
Library), 29l (Pictor International/ImageState), 47tl (Robert Harding
World Imagery/Robert Harding Picture Library Ltd), 60tr (Joseph
Lawrence Name), 60tl (Pictor International/ImageState), 62l (Janine
Wiedel/Janine Wiedel Photo library), 77t (Justin Kase), 78l (Andre
Jenny), 87b (Pictor International/ImageState), 88cl (don jon red);
Alton Towers p13c; Anthony Blake Photo Library p38 (1-4, 6, 7);
BALTIC The Centre for Contemporary Art pp40r (Etienne Clement),
41 (Elliott Young); Cadmium p58tl; Camelot Group Plc p67tr; Canon
(UK) Ltd p12b; Corbis UK Ltd. pp8c (Paul Thompson/Ecoscene),
8/9 (David Turnley), 8l (John Madere), 9r (Tom Nebbia), 10cr, 11
(Bohemian Nomad Picturemakers), 14 (Robert Essel NYC), 16br
(Rune Hellestad), 16bl (Rune Hellestad), 18, 22t (Michelle Chaplow),
22b (Kim Sayer), 27b, 27tr (James Marshall), 29tr (Adrian Arbib),
30b (Tom Bean), 30t (Paul A. Souders), 32c (Duomo), 32/33 (Jay
Dickman), 34b (Bob Krist), 38h (Owen Franken), 40l, 47c, 47b
(James L. Amos), 48t, 48c (Neal Preston), 51tl (Charles Jean Marc
Sygma), 51bl, 51cl (RNT Productions), 51c (Richard Hamilton Smith),
55r (Bettmann), 58cl (Raymond Gehman), 58bl, 58r, 60tc, 60bl,
60bcl, 62/63, 63r (Chuck Savage), 67tl (Stephanie Maze), 68t
(Fotografia, Inc.), 77b (Ron Watts), 80cl, 80tl (Barry Lewis), 80tr
(Stuart Hughes), 87tc, 87tr, 88l (Adam Woolfitt), 90l (Roger
Ressmeyer), 90/91 (Helen King), 91r (Bill Varie), 92, 94r (Mark L
Stephenson), 96b, 96/97 (Tom Brakefield), 100, 102 (Mug Shots);
Empics pp36/37 (DPA), 42; Fujifilm UK Limited p12t; Getty Images
pp67b (Inc. Janeart/The Image Bank), 68b (Taxi), 93t (Ezra
Shaw/Allsport), 119l (Stone), 119r (Taxi); Gordon Ramsay Scholar
p38b; Kobal Collection p54/55; Oxford University Press pp7r
(Harrods), 35t, 35c, 35b, 38 (5) (Philip Hargraves), 48b, 52 (Helen
Wendholt), 98; Photos taken by expedition photographers courtesy of
Raleigh International p56/57(all); Press Association p13t (David
Davies); Remarkable (Pencils) Ltd p28; Rex Features pp10cl (Julian
Makey), 10cc (Peter Brooker), pp10t (Eugene Adebari), 10b (Sipa
Press),
16cr, 16tr (Richard Young), 16cl (Richard Young), 16tl, 29br (Action
Press), 32b (Sipa Press), 33r (Action Press), 34t (Laurent Baheux),
36l (Jeremy Durkin), 47tr (David Hurrell), 53 (Ray Tang), 78r (Action
Press), 80cr (Dan Charity), 87tl (Anders Krusberg), 88cr (Action
Press), 88tr (Frank Monaco), 93b (Sipa Press), 94l (Randy Bauer),
95r (I.B.L.); Rob Carter Photography p72; Sally & Richard Greenhill
pp60br, 80b; Tim Street Porter © House & Garden/The Condé Nast
Publications Ltd pp7l, 20, 21; The Nobel Foundation p95l; Zooid
Pictures pp67tc (Dan Sinclair), 94c (Dan Sinclair);

Illustrations by: Ian Dicks pp13 (phone), 16, 75, 81, 103, 126, 128, 129,
130, 131, 132, 133, 135; Mark Duffin pp19, 40, 51, 58, 74, 82, 98;
David Eaton pp59, 71, 79; Spike Gerrell pp7, 24, 25, 44, 46, 64, 65,
76, 84, 85, 99, 104, 105; Ned Jolliffe pp13 (job), 30, 31, 32, 50, 100;
Sparky (Tim Kahane) pp43, 70; Jan McCafferty pp73, 83; Lee
Woodgate pp15, 17, 20, 48, 77, 89